FASCINATING FACTS

Exploring the Myths and Mysteries of
JUDAISM

SINAI
SCHOLARS
SOCIETY

וַיִּקְרָא ה׳ אֶל שְׁמוּאֵל
וַיֹּאמֶר הִנֵּנִי
—שמואל א ג:ד—

God called out to Shmuel,
and he responded,
"Here I am (*Hineni*)!"
—I Samuel 3:4

"Hineni!"
"This is how the pious respond to God's calling,
with humility and readiness."
—Rashi, Genesis 22:1

In the wake of the Holocaust,
as the Jewish People rose from the ruins and the ashes,

Mr. Shmuel (Sami) Rohr, of blessed memory,

heard God's calling. His response was a resounding *"Hineni!"*
With humility, selflessness, determination, and peerless commitment,
he established a family and served as a leading protagonist
in the renaissance of *Klal Yisrael* around the world.

THIS COURSE IS LOVINGLY DEDICATED
TO THE MEMORY OF

Mr. Shmuel (Sami) Rohr

ר׳ שמואל ב״ר יהושע אליהו ז״ל

PATRON AND BENEFACTOR OF MULTITUDES
OF TORAH INSTITUTIONS THE WORLD OVER
WHO PASSED AWAY ON

י״ז מנחם אב, ה׳תשע״ב
August 5, 2012

May the Torah study undertaken in his memory
by many thousands of JLI students worldwide,
whose study is inspired by his vision and generosity,
grant much nachas and menuchah to his neshamah
and be a source of comfort and inspiration to his esteemed family
who carry on his legacy with gezunt and menuchah.

לזכרון ולעילוי נשמת

ר׳ שמואל ב״ר יהושע אליהו ז״ל
ראהר

תנצב״ה

Endorsements for Fascinating Facts

"As a teacher of Jewish adults, my responsibility is not only to convey knowledge, but also to help students unlearn and rethink their Judaism. Doing this—through the study of this intriguing course—they can potentially transform themselves, their families, and their communities."

Betsy Dolgin Katz, Ed.D.
Adjunct Professor, Spertus Institute of Jewish Studies and Gratz College
Author of *The Adult Jewish Education Handbook* and *Reinventing Adult Jewish Learning*

"The JLI series of courses continues to be of high caliber with a judicious use of Jewish primary texts to facilitate study and discussion. Each volume is a fascinating exploration of a theme, bringing the corpus of Jewish learning into the conversation from every generation of Jewish learning and spanning—literally—more than three thousand years. I salute Chabad for soliciting and dedicating extensive resources to create and promote the Jewish Learning Institute, among the most significant Jewish adult and teen educational endeavors offered in our Jewish community."

Rabbi Eric M. Lankin, D.Min.
Chief, Institutional Advancement and Education Jewish National Fund

"*Kol Hakavod* to the Rohr Jewish Learning Institute for this valuable addition to the curriculum. Jewish culture, with books being its oldest and foremost component, is rich in beautiful traditions. *Fascinating Facts: Exploring the Myths and Mysteries of Judaism* goes a long way toward enriching our understanding and clarifying the meaning of many of the traditions we hold dear. It will deepen the knowledge for the informed Jew and provide an entrée for those with less background."

Carolyn Starman Hessel
Director, Jewish Book Council

"I commend the Rohr Jewish Learning Institute on its new curriculum *Fascinating Facts: Exploring the Myths and Mysteries of Judaism*. This highly professional curriculum offers much more than a collection of readings, explanations, and discussion points. In each sentence, it connects with each learner's inner spark of curiosity about the universe and about being Jewish and then opens up new and profound worlds of knowledge and experience from within the depths of Jewish tradition. Judaism is not presented here as a cute titillating riddle that challenges the Jewish learner to find a solution, but rather as a precious gift that is offered lovingly, sensitively, and joyfully for ongoing spiritual, social, and existential enrichment. The pedagogical approach here is itself an enactment of the Jewish values that the curriculum seeks to inspire in the learner."

Daniel Marom, Ph.D.
Academic Director, Mandel Leadership Institute Jerusalem, Israel

"How often do we hear misconceptions about the rich Jewish tradition from people whose own Jewish background was limited to an elementary education? This wonderful approach to learning is designed to engage curious adults in exploring the basics of our tradition that are so often misconstrued and fills a much-needed void in the adult learning field. Raising the questions and providing accurate and thoughtful responses will encourage even greater learning in the future."

Paul A. Flexner, Ed.D.
Assistant Professor, Georgia State University
Department of Educational Psychology and
Special Education

"The JLI course *Fascinating Facts* is the sort of entertaining crash course we all wish we had stumbled upon years ago. For someone looking for a broadband download of millennia of wisdom, this is one of the best places to start."

Lawrence Kelemen
Professor of Education, Neve Yerushalayim
College of Jewish Studies for Women
Author of *Permission to Believe*
and *Permission to Receive*

Table of Contents

Lesson 1

The Story of Your Life
How to Read the Torah

Introduction

It's time for a new reading of the Bible. We will start by picking out the bad apples and end by discovering who shattered something whole to fix what was broken. In between, we'll face justice eye to eye and find out what Jews did before they learned to quote chapter and verse.

I. Myths and Misconceptions

A. A Tale of Two Trees

Learning Interaction 1

When Adam and Eve sinned by eating from the Tree of Knowledge, what fruit did they eat?

a. Apple

b. Fig

c. Grape

d. Orange

וַיַּצְמַח ה׳ אֱלֹקִים מִן הָאֲדָמָה כָּל עֵץ נֶחְמָד לְמַרְאֶה וְטוֹב לְמַאֲכָל, וְעֵץ הַחַיִּים בְּתוֹךְ הַגָּן וְעֵץ הַדַּעַת טוֹב וָרָע . . .

וַיְצַו ה׳ אֱלֹקִים עַל הָאָדָם לֵאמֹר, "מִכֹּל עֵץ הַגָּן אָכֹל תֹּאכֵל. וּמֵעֵץ הַדַּעַת טוֹב וָרָע לֹא תֹאכַל מִמֶּנּוּ, כִּי בְּיוֹם אֲכָלְךָ מִמֶּנּוּ מוֹת תָּמוּת."

בראשית ב,ט–יז

The Lord God caused to sprout from the ground every tree that was pleasant to see and good to eat, and, in the midst of the garden, the Tree of Life and the Tree of Knowledge of Good and Evil. . . .

And the Lord God commanded man, saying, "Of every tree of the garden you may freely eat. But of the Tree of Knowledge of Good and Evil you shall not eat, for you shall surely die on the day that you eat thereof."

Genesis 2:9–17

אילן שאכל ממנו אדם הראשון:

רבי מאיר אומר גפן היה . . .

רבי נחמיה אומר תאנה היתה . . .

רבי יהודה אומר חטה היתה.

תלמוד בבלי, ברכות מ,א

Babylonian Talmud. A literary work of monumental proportions that draws upon the legal, spiritual, intellectual, ethical, and historical traditions of Judaism. The 37 tractates of the Babylonian Talmud contain the teachings of the Jewish sages from the period after the destruction of the 2nd Temple through the 5th century CE. It has served as the primary vehicle for the transmission of the Oral Law and the education of Jews over the centuries; it is the entry point for all subsequent legal, ethical, and theological Jewish scholarship.

The tree from which Adam ate:

Rabbi Meir says it was a grapevine. . . .

Rabbi Nechemiah says it was a fig tree. . . .

Rabbi Yehudah says it was a wheat stalk.

Talmud, Berachot 40a

Question for Discussion

Can you think of biblical clues to support any of these positions?

Text 3 📜

רבי עזריה ורבי יהודה בר סימון בשם רבי יהושע בן לוי אמר: "חס ושלום! לא גלה
הקדוש ברוך הוא אותו אילן לאדם, ולא עתיד לגלותו . . . ואם על כבוד תולדותיו חס
המקום, על כבודו על אחת כמה וכמה, אתמהא".

בראשית רבה טו,ז

Rabbi Azariah and Rabbi Yehudah ben Simon said in the name of Rabbi Yehoshua ben Levi: "Heaven forbid! God never revealed the identity of the tree to any man, and He never will. . . . If God is anxious to safeguard the dignity of the average human being, how much more so the dignity of Adam and Chavah!

Midrash, Bereishit Rabah 15:7

Bereishit Rabah is an early rabbinic commentary on the Book of Genesis, bearing the name of Rabbi Oshiya Rabah (Rabbi Oshiya "the Great") whose teaching opens this work. This Midrash provides textual exegeses and anecdotes, expounds upon the biblical narrative, and develops and illustrates moral principles. It was produced by the sages of the Talmud in the Land of Israel; it is thought to be the earliest non-halachic Midrash still extant. It was first published in Constantinople in 1512 together with four other Midrashic works on the other four books of the Pentateuch.

Text 4a 📜

וַיֵּרָא מַלְאַךְ ה' אֵלָיו בְּלַבַּת אֵשׁ מִתּוֹךְ הַסְּנֶה. וַיַּרְא, וְהִנֵּה הַסְּנֶה בֹּעֵר בָּאֵשׁ וְהַסְּנֶה
אֵינֶנּוּ אֻכָּל.

שמות ג,ב

An angel of God appeared to [Moses] in the heart of a fire in the midst of the thornbush. Moses looked, and, behold, the thornbush was ablaze, but the thornbush was not consumed.

Exodus 3:2

Text 4b 📜

"בְּכָל צָרָתָם לוֹ צָר" (תהילים צא,טו). אָמַר לוֹ הַקָּדוֹשׁ בָּרוּךְ הוּא לְמֹשֶׁה, "אִי אַתָּה מַרְגִּישׁ שֶׁאֲנִי שָׁרוּי בְּצַעַר כְּשֵׁם שֶׁיִּשְׂרָאֵל שְׁרוּיִים בְּצַעַר, הֱוֵי יוֹדֵעַ מִמָּקוֹם שֶׁאֲנִי מְדַבֵּר עִמְּךָ, מִתּוֹךְ הַקּוֹצִים". כִּבְיָכוֹל, "אֲנִי שׁוּתָּף בְּצַעֲרָן".

שמות רבה ב,ה

❝ am with [Israel] in their distress" (Psalms 91:15). God said to Moses, "Do you not realize that I am distressed just as the Jewish people are distressed [in their bondage]? Take note from whence I am communicating with you—from within the thornbush." As if to say, "I am a partner in their distress."

Midrash, Shemot Rabah 2:5

Shemot Rabah is an early rabbinic commentary of the Book of Exodus. This Midrash, written mostly in Hebrew, provides textual exegeses and narratives, expounds upon the biblical narrative, and develops and illustrates moral principles. It was first published in Constantinople in 1512 together with four other midrashic works on the other four books of the Pentateuch.

Question for Discussion

Let us now take a step back and analyze the two Midrashic texts. One passage said that the Tree of Knowledge shouldn't be known; the other explained why the Torah specifies the kind of shrub in which the angel of God spoke to Moses. What does this tell us about how the Midrash regards the stories of the Torah?

Text 5

ווי להההוא בר נש דאמר דהא אורייתא אתא לאחזאה ספורין בעלמא ומלין דהדיוטי

... אי לאחזאה מלה דעלמא, אפילו אינון קפסירי דעלמא אית ביניהו מלין עלאין

יתיר, אי הכי נזיל אבתרייהו ונעביד מנייהו אורייתא כהאי גוונא!

זוהר ג, קנב,א

Woe to the person who says that the Torah's objective is merely to relate stories and mundane tales. . . . If the objective of the Torah were to relate historical matters, the rulers of the world have historical chronicles that are superior; let us utilize them and produce from them a [better] Torah!

Zohar 3:152a

Zohar. The seminal work of Kabbalah, Jewish mysticism. It is a mystical commentary on the Torah, written in Aramaic and Hebrew. According to Arizal, the Zohar consists of the teachings of Rabbi Shimon bar Yocha'i who lived in Israel during the 2nd century CE. The Zohar has become one of the indispensable texts of traditional Judaism, alongside and nearly equal in stature to the Mishnah and Talmud.

B. Squaring the Tablets

Learning Interaction 2

Have you ever seen a depiction of the tablets upon which the Ten Commandments were written? Can you draw them?

Text 6

ארון שעשה משה, אמתים וחצי ארכו, ואמה וחצי רחבו, ואמה וחצי קומתו . . .
והלוחות, ארכן ששה, ורחבן ששה, ועביין שלשה, מונחות כנגד ארכו של ארון.

תלמוד בבלי, בבא בתרא יד,א

The ark that Moses constructed was two and a half cubits in length, one and a half cubits in width, and one and a half cubits in height. . . . Each of the tablets was six [handbreadths] long, six [handbreadths] wide, and three [handbreadths] deep, lying along the length of the ark.

Talmud, Baba Batra 14a

Question for Discussion

Does this text support or negate the possibility of the tablets having rounded tops?

Text 7 🕮

הלוחות היו מרובעות, ששה טפחים באורך וששה טפחים ברוחב . . . ואם תשכיל
עוד במדת הלוחות בין אורך ורוחב ועובי, תמצא כי היה בכל לוח ולוח מאה
ושמונה טפחים.

רבינו בחיי, שמות לא,יח

The tablets were square: six handbreadths long and six handbreadths wide. . . . If you study the dimensions of the tablets—the height, width, and depth—you will find that each tablet contained 108 cubic handbreadths.

Rabbi Bachaye ben Asher, Exodus 31:18

Rabbi Bachaye ben Asher (ca. 1255–1340). Author of a Torah commentary, *Midrash Rabbeinu Bachaye*. He was born in Saragossa, Spain, and is known for systemizing the 4 classic levels of exegesis: *peshat* (plain meaning), *remez* (allusive meaning), *derash* (homiletic exposition), and *sod* (Kabbalistic meaning). He also authored *Kad Hakemach*, a work on ethics.

Figure 1.1

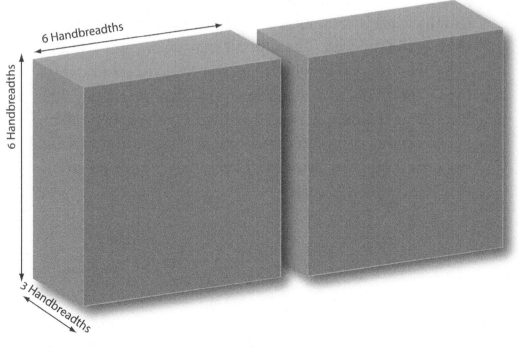

6 Handbreadths

6 Handbreadths

3 Handbreadths

6×6×3=108

Text 8

Rabbi Ari Z. Zivotofsky, PhD. Scientist, columnist, and historian. Rabbi Dr. Zivotofsky is a senior lecturer at Bar Ilan University's Brain Science Program. He has earned advanced degrees in electrical engineering, math, and Jewish history, and has worked to collect Jewish traditions from far-flung Jewish communities for 20 years. He writes a regular column in *Jewish Action* magazine.

The current standard perception of the Tablets derives from Christian art. . . . In Italy, from ancient times through Romanesque and Gothic periods and up until the 16th century, the *Luchot* were portrayed as two rectangular tablets. In France, from at least the 12th century, it was the familiar rounded form that at a certain point supplanted all the other forms; so much so that from the 16th century on it is almost impossible to find Tablets represented in any other fashion.

Scholars have traced the origin of this form with relative ease. There are several features that almost always go together that betray its source. When portrayed as rectangular, the Tablets are always separate. When they have a rounded top, they are usually adjacent and even attached. Furthermore, when rounded they usually have a frame. All of these indicate a familiar form—the diptych. The diptych was an ancient writing tablet having two hinged leaves that was used in various forms through the Middle Ages. Representing the Luchot as a diptych lies in its use as a writing tablet, and probably originated in England, where the earliest extant example of rounded *Luchot* can be found in an 11th century manuscript.

Rabbi Ari Z. Zivotofsky, "What's the Truth about . . . the Luchot?" *Jewish Action*, Summer 1998

Figure 1.2

1. I am Hashem your God.	6. You shall not murder.
2. You shall have no other God beside me.	7. You shall not commit adultery.
3. You shall not take the name of Hashem in vain.	8. You shall not steal.
4. Remember the Shabbat, to keep it holy.	9. You shall not bear false witness against your neighbor.
5. Honor your father and your mother.	10. You shall not covet your neighbor's wife.

C. Moses' Horns

Text 9a

וַיְהִי בְּרֶדֶת מֹשֶׁה מֵהַר סִינַי וּשְׁנֵי לֻחֹת הָעֵדֻת בְּיַד מֹשֶׁה בְּרִדְתּוֹ מִן הָהָר, וּמֹשֶׁה לֹא יָדַע כִּי קָרַן עוֹר פָּנָיו בְּדַבְּרוֹ אִתּוֹ. וַיַּרְא אַהֲרֹן וְכָל בְּנֵי יִשְׂרָאֵל אֶת מֹשֶׁה וְהִנֵּה קָרַן עוֹר פָּנָיו, וַיִּירְאוּ מִגֶּשֶׁת אֵלָיו.

שמות לד,כט-ל

When Moses descended from Mount Sinai, the two tablets of the testimony were in his hand as he descended from the mountain. And Moses did not know that the skin of his face had become radiant (*karan*) when [God] spoke with him. Aaron and all the children of Israel saw Moses and, behold, the skin of his face was radiant, and they were afraid to approach him.

Exodus 34:29–30

Text **9b** 📖

When Moses came down from Mount Sinai, he held the two tablets of the testimony, and he knew not that his face was horned from the conversation of the Lord.

Vulgate, Exodus 34:29

Jerome (ca. 337–420), the most learned student of the Bible among the Latin ecclesiastical writers, and, until modern times, the only Christian scholar able to study the Hebrew Bible in the original. His knowledge of Hebrew appears especially in his chief work, the Latin translation of the Bible from the Hebrew original, the Vulgate. No friend of the Jews, he often reproached them for being stiff-necked, dissented with their views in the strongest terms, and reveled in their misfortune.

Text **10** 📖

מקום שבעלי תשובה עומדין צדיקים גמורים אינם עומדין.
תלמוד בבלי, ברכות לד,ב

The heights achieved by those who repent cannot be attained even by those who are perfectly righteous.

Talmud, Berachot 34b

Question **for Discussion**

Can you justify this Talmudic statement?

D. Chapter and Verse

Optional Section

Text 11

ראיתי לחלק כל חלק כל ספר וספר מהם אל פרשיות, אבל לא יהיו ארוכות וגדולות . . . וגם לא יהיו קטנות וקצרות כמו שעשאם החכם גירונימ"ו אשר העתיק ספרי הקדש לנוצרים, שעשה בספר יהושע כ"ד פרשיות, ובספר שופטים כ"א פרשיות, ובספר שמואל ל"ה.

אברבנאל, הקדמה לנביאים ראשונים

decided to divide each book into sections. However, they will not be very long . . . nor will they be very short chapters, like [the chapters of] the scholar Hieronymus, who translated the holy Scriptures for the Christians and divided the book of Joshua into twenty-four chapters, the book of Judges into twenty-one chapters, and the book of Samuel into thirty-five chapters.

Rabbi Don Yitschak Abarbanel, Introduction to the Early Prophets

Question for Discussion

If the chapter-and-verse system emanated from Christian sources, why have Jews not refrained from adopting this system?

II. The Oral Torah

A. Help Needed!

Learning Interaction 3

The following paragraph is taken from the Shema (Deuteronomy 6:5–9).

Y ou shall love the Lord, your God, with all your heart and with all your soul, and with all your means. And these words that I command you this day shall be upon your heart. You shall teach them to your sons and speak of them when you sit in your house, when you walk on the way, when you lie down, and when you rise up. And you shall bind them for a sign upon your hand, and they shall be for *totafot* between your eyes. And you shall inscribe them upon the doorposts of your house and upon your gates."

Divest yourself of any knowledge you may already have regarding the nature of the *mitzvot* referred to in this passage (which is all a product of the oral interpretation). Relying only on your careful reading of the text, try to answer these questions:

a.   **What are "these words that I command you today"?**

b.   **How do we place them on our heart?**

c.   **How do we bind them to our hand?**

d.   **How do we make them into *totafot* between our eyes?**

e.   **How do we inscribe them on our doorposts and on our gates?**

B. Internal Evidence

Text **12a**

וְזָבַחְתָּ מִבְּקָרְךָ וּמִצֹּאנְךָ אֲשֶׁר נָתַן ה' לְךָ כַּאֲשֶׁר צִוִּיתִךָ, וְאָכַלְתָּ בִּשְׁעָרֶיךָ בְּכֹל אַוַּת נַפְשֶׁךָ.

דברים יב,כ-כא

You shall slaughter, as I have commanded you, of your cattle and of your sheep that God has given you, and you may eat [meat] in your cities as per your hearts' desire.

Deuteronomy 12:20–21

Text 12b

זביחה זו האמורה בתורה סתם צריך לפרש אותה ולידע: באי זה מקום מן הבהמה
שוחטין? וכמה שיעור השחיטה? ובאי זה דבר שוחטין? ומתי שוחטין? והיכן שוחטין?
וכיצד שוחטין? ומה הן הדברים המפסידין את השחיטה? ומי הוא השוחט?
ועל כל הדברים האלו צונו בתורה ואמר, "וזבחת מבקרך וגו' כאשר צויתיך ואכלת
בשעריך וגו'", שכל הדברים האלו על פה צוה בהן כשאר תורה שבעל פה.

משנה תורה, הלכות שחיטה א,ד

The slaughter that the Torah mentions, without any elaboration, needs to be explained in order for us to know the following: Which place on the animal is [appropriate] for ritual slaughter? How large must the incision be? With what do we slaughter? When do we slaughter? Where do we slaughter? How do we slaughter? What factors disqualify the slaughter? Who can slaughter?

Regarding all these factors, the Torah instructs us: "You shall slaughter, as I commanded you, of your cattle. . . ." All of these laws were commanded to us orally, as is true with regard to the remainder of the Oral Law.

Maimonides, *Mishneh Torah*, Laws of Ritual Slaughter 1:4

Rabbi Moshe ben Maimon (Maimonides/Rambam, 1135–1204). Halachic authority, philosopher, author, and physician. Maimonides was born in Cordoba, Spain. After the conquest of Cordoba by the Almohads, he fled Spain and eventually settled in Cairo, Egypt. There, he became the leader of the Jewish community and served as court physician to the vizier of Egypt. He is most noted for authoring the *Mishneh Torah*, an encyclopedic arrangement of Jewish law, and for his philosophical work, *Guide for the Perplexed*. His rulings on Jewish law are considered integral to the formation of halachic consensus.

C. An Eye for an Eye

Text 13 📜

עַיִן תַּחַת עַיִן, שֵׁן תַּחַת שֵׁן, יָד תַּחַת יָד, רֶגֶל תַּחַת רָגֶל. כְּוִיָה תַּחַת כְּוִיָה, פֶּצַע תַּחַת
פָּצַע, חַבּוּרָה תַּחַת חַבּוּרָה.

שמות כא,כד-כה

An eye for an eye, a tooth for a tooth, a hand for a hand, a foot for a foot. A burn for a burn, a wound for a wound, a bruise for a bruise.

Exodus 21:24–25

Learning Interaction 4

Together with a partner, read Texts 14a and 14b and then answer the questions below:

Text 14a 📜

וְכִי יְרִיבֻן אֲנָשִׁים וְהִכָּה אִישׁ אֶת רֵעֵהוּ בְּאֶבֶן אוֹ בְאֶגְרֹף, וְלֹא יָמוּת וְנָפַל לְמִשְׁכָּב, אִם
יָקוּם וְהִתְהַלֵּךְ בַּחוּץ עַל מִשְׁעַנְתּוֹ וְנִקָּה הַמַּכֶּה, רַק שִׁבְתּוֹ יִתֵּן וְרַפֹּא יְרַפֵּא.

שם, כא,יח-יט

If men quarrel and one strikes the other with a stone or with a fist, and [the victim] does not die but is confined to bed, if [the victim] then gets up and walks about outside unaided, the assailant shall be cleared; he shall only pay for [income lost due to the victim's enforced] idleness and his medical costs.

Ibid., 21:18–19

Text **14b** 📖

וְלֹא תִקְחוּ כֹפֶר לְנֶפֶשׁ רֹצֵחַ אֲשֶׁר הוּא רָשָׁע לָמוּת, כִּי מוֹת יוּמָת. וְלֹא תִקְחוּ כֹפֶר לָנוּס
אֶל עִיר מִקְלָטוֹ לָשׁוּב לָשֶׁבֶת בָּאָרֶץ עַד מוֹת הַכֹּהֵן.

במדבר לה,לא-לב

You shall not accept ransom for the life of a murderer who is guilty of death, for he shall be put to death. You shall not accept ransom for one who has fled to his city of refuge, to allow him to return to live in the land, before the *kohen* has died.

Numbers 35:31–32

According to your analysis, Text 14a

a. assumes that "an eye for an eye" is literal.

b. assumes that "an eye for an eye" is not literal.

c. has no relevance to the subject.

According to your analysis, Text 14b

a. assumes that "an eye for an eye" is literal.

b. assumes that "an eye for an eye" is not literal.

c. has no relevance to the subject.

וּמַכֵּה נֶפֶשׁ בְּהֵמָה יְשַׁלְּמֶנָּה, נֶפֶשׁ תַּחַת נָפֶשׁ.

ויקרא כד,יח

One who slays an animal [that belongs to another] shall pay for it: a life for a life.

Leviticus 24:18

Question for Discussion

What does "a life for a life" mean in this context?

III. The Parting Lesson

Learning Interaction 5

What was Moses' greatest feat, his most defining achievement?

a.   **Confronting Pharaoh**

b.   **Splitting the Red Sea**

c.   **Transmitting the Torah to the Jews**

d.   **Breaking the tablets**

e.   **Other**

Text 16a

וְלֹא קָם נָבִיא עוֹד בְּיִשְׂרָאֵל כְּמֹשֶׁה אֲשֶׁר יְדָעוֹ ה' פָּנִים אֶל פָּנִים. לְכָל הָאֹתוֹת וְהַמּוֹפְתִים
אֲשֶׁר שְׁלָחוֹ ה' לַעֲשׂוֹת בְּאֶרֶץ מִצְרָיִם לְפַרְעֹה וּלְכָל עֲבָדָיו וּלְכָל אַרְצוֹ. וּלְכֹל הַיָּד הַחֲזָקָה
וּלְכֹל הַמּוֹרָא הַגָּדוֹל אֲשֶׁר עָשָׂה מֹשֶׁה לְעֵינֵי כָּל יִשְׂרָאֵל.

דברים לד, י-יב

There has never arisen another prophet in Israel like Moses, who communicated with God face to face; [who executed] all the signs and wonders that God sent him to perform in the land of Egypt upon Pharaoh and all his servants, and to all his land; and for all the strong hand and great awesomeness performed by Moses before the eyes of all of Israel.

Deuteronomy 34:10–12

Question for Discussion

Is this a fitting eulogy for Moses? Is this a worthy ending to the entire Torah?

Rabbi Shlomo Yitschaki (Rashi, 1040–1105). Most noted biblical and Talmudic commentator. Born in Troyes, France, Rashi studied in the famed *yeshivot* of Mainz and Worms. His commentaries on the Pentateuch and the Talmud, which focus on the simple understanding of the text, are considered the most fundamental of all the commentaries that preceded and followed. Since their initial printings, the commentaries have appeared in virtually every edition of the Talmud and Bible. Many of the famed authors of the *Tosafot* are among Rashi's descendants.

Text 16b

שנשאו לבו לשבור הלוחות לעיניהם, שנאמר (דברים ט,יז), "ואשברם לעיניכם".
רש"י, שם

This expression alludes to the incident in which [Moses] was inspired to smash the tablets before [Israel's] eyes, as is stated (Deuteronomy 9:17), "And I shattered them before your eyes."

Rashi, ad loc.

Question for Discussion

Is this a fitting conclusion to Moses' eulogy? Is this a worthy ending to the entire Torah?

Learning Interaction 6

Why did Moses break the tablets?

a. They simply fell

b. Because he was angry

c. Because the Jews were undeserving of receiving them

d. To destroy thereby the golden calf

e. Out of his love for the Jewish people

f. He wanted to impress upon the people the severity of their sin

Text 17 ▌

למה הדבר דומה, למלך ששלח לקדש אשה עם הסרסור, הלך הסרסור לעשות
שליחות המלך וקלקלה עם אחר. הסרסור שהיה נקי מה עשה? נטל את כתובתה מה
שנתן לו המלך לקדשה, וקרעה. אמר, "מוטב שתדון כפנויה ולא כאשת איש".
כך עשה משה: כיון שעשו ישראל אותו מעשה, נטל את הלוחות ושיברן.

שמות רבה מג,א

This is like a king who sent an agent to betroth a woman on his behalf. The agent executed the king's order, and the [now-betrothed] woman proceeded to engage in an adulterous affair. What did the agent do? He ripped up the betrothal contract that the king had given him. "Better," he reasoned, "that she should be judged as an unbetrothed woman, and not as a betrothed one."

Moses did the same: When the Jews committed that terrible act, he took the tablets and broke them.

Midrash, *Shemot Rabah* 43:1

Question for Discussion

According to this Midrash, why did Moses break the tablets?

Lesson Summary

1. According to Jewish tradition, it would be incorrect to identify the fruit of the Tree of Knowledge as an apple.

2. In the Jewish view, our failings and shortcomings should not be on our minds at all times. Only at specific times is one supposed to think of past failings and focus on repentance. The rest of life should be dedicated to moving on.

3. We are supposed to be careful about sharing unnecessary negative information about others. When someone strays, it's by no means an excuse for others to deprive him or her of dignity and privacy.

4. The Torah specifies that the "burning bush" was a thornbush, generally translated as the thorny shrub called *rubus sanctus*.

5. When human beings experience suffering, God reassures them that He is present in their pain and sorrow; He is not an indifferent bystander.

6. A careful reading of Midrash demonstrates that it regards the details and omissions in the Torah as teaching important lessons about life. The English word "bible" means "book," but the Hebrew word "Torah" suggests instruction and guidance—an instruction manual for life.

7. Whenever we open a Torah, we ought to delve deeply into each story, chapter, verse, and word, to find the meaningful messages and personal relevance embedded within them.

8. The Talmud states that the *Luchot* were not rectangular but square. It also seems to imply that they were not arched at the top.

9. The Ten Commandments have two general themes. The first five, engraved on the first tablet, are laws between man and God; the latter five, engraved on the second tablet, are laws between human beings.

10. The fact that the Ten Commandments include both religious and social laws teaches us that, in Judaism, there is no divide between these two realms. Both are important; both should complement each other.

11. The myth of Jews with horns comes from a mistaken biblical translation. Moses' face was glowing and radiant; the Vulgate translated this as "horned."

12. It is from our failures that we can experience the most profound growth. A penitent demonstrates greater commitment and dedication by going against his or her nature.

13. The chapter-and-verse system widely in use today has come to us from Christian sources. In order to perform effectively during forced debates, Jews needed to use the same system as their Christian counterparts.

14. The Jews who received the Torah from Moses also relied upon interpretation—the interpretation that Moses received from God, which was then transmitted from generation to generation in the form of the Oral Torah. We have internal biblical evidence for the existence of the Oral Law.

15. The Oral Law states that "an eye for an eye" means that an assailant must pay a monetary fine. That this was the intention of the verse can be demonstrated from within the written Torah itself.

16. A person's physical body corresponds to and has evolved from various non-physical attributes within the divine. Hurting another is an assault on a person created in the very image of God.

17. According to Rashi, the closing words of the Torah suggest that Moses' defining moment was the destruction of the tablets. This incident highlighted his love for the Jewish people as well as the fact that without the people, the Torah has no value.

Additional Readings

What's the Truth about ... the Translation of Yam Suf?

by **Rabbi Dr. Ari Zivotofsky**

MISCONCEPTION: Upon leaving Egypt, the Jews crossed the *Yam Suf*, which is translated as the Red Sea. This translation, however, is an error. Red Sea is a corruption of the correct Old English (OE) translation, Reed (Rede) Sea. (Rede is a legitimate spelling of reed in OE.)

FACT: The notion that the Yam Suf is the modern-day Red Sea predates any English translation of the Bible by well over a thousand years. In fact, it seems that until the late eighteenth century no one questioned the translation and identification of Yam Suf with the Red Sea.[1]

Red Sea is the ancient and preferred translation of Yam Suf. While some believe that *suf* refers to reed-like plants growing in or near the sea and that literal translations of proper nouns in the Bible are preferable, Reed Sea remains a questionable translation at best. Unfortunately, the notion that Yam Suf should be translated as "Reed Sea" and not "Red Sea" seems to be gaining in popularity.[2]

BACKGROUND: Determining the "correct" translation of Yam Suf is not simply a matter of ascertaining the meaning of the words. Rather, several issues need to be addressed: Is the body of water that is today called the Red Sea the one that was split for the Israelites to pass through? Irrespective of the location, is Reed Sea an accurate translation of Yam Suf? Assuming Reed Sea *is* the literal translation of Yam Suf, does that make it the *correct* translation? Every one of these separate but inter-dependent questions needs to be looked at, although not every question has a complete and satisfactory answer.

The name Yam Suf appears in Tanach a total of twenty-three times.[3] However, most people associate Yam Suf with the body of water the Israelites crossed while fleeing Egypt. Many of the sources that translate Yam Suf as Red Sea indicate that literally it means "Sea of Reeds or Rushes" (see, for example, *The Interpreter's Dictionary of the Bible*[4] [1962, vol. 4, pp. 19-21]). In Exodus 13:18, when describing the Jews fleeing Egypt, the Torah states: "God took the people in a roundabout path . . . to the Yam Suf." ArtScroll's Stone Edition Chumash translates Yam Suf as Sea of Reeds and includes a note stating that what is today known as the Red Sea is situated too far south for the Jews to have crossed it upon fleeing Egypt. The Jewish Publication Society Tanakh simply calls it the Sea of Reeds, and the Koren Chumash calls it the Sea of Suf with no attempt at translation or identification.

In order to determine which body of water Yam Suf is referring to, it is important to look for parallels in Tanach. The Hebrew word spelled *samach-vav-peh* can be read either as *suf* or as *sof*, i.e., the Sea of Suf or the Sea of Sof,[5] depending upon whether the vav is vocalized as a *shuruk* (*suf*) or a *cholam* (*sof*). Ibn Ezra (Exodus 13:18) states that some read the word as *sof* and explain that it is called Yam Sof because it lies at the end of the world[6]; however, he claims, that this is a "big error" because "the Yam Sof is not at the end [of the world]; the Atlantic Ocean is at the end." The correct reading, he asserts, is *suf*. Rashi (Exodus 13:18) explains that *suf*

---

[1] See *Encyclopeda Mikrait*, vol. 3, 695-699, s.v. Yam Suf.

[2] See e.g., *Schottenstein Edition Talmud Bavli, Sotah* 11a, no. 36, 39 and 61.

[3] For example: Exodus 13:18; 15:4; 15:22; 23:31; Numbers 14:25; 21:4; 33:10; 33:11; Deuteronomy 1:40; 2:1; 11:4; Joshua 2:10; 4:23; 24:6; Shoftim 11:16; I Kings 9:26; Psalms 106:7, 9, 22; 136:13, 15; Nechamiah 9:9; and Jeremiah 49:21.

[4] The translators of this work are so convinced of the accuracy of this translation, they wrote (p. 20): "Luther, who relied on the Hebrew, rendered *Yam Sûph* correctly by calling it *Schilfmeer*, 'Sea of Reeds.'"

[5] In Judges 11:16, the Septuagint (Manuscript B) has Yam Siph.

[6] That the world has an "end" is not a strange idea. See e.g., Daniel 4:8: "that its sight was to the end (*sof*) of the earth."

in Yam Suf is similar to "*agam*," which means a pond, in that it has reeds (*kanim*) growing in it. Expounding on Rashi, Siftei Chachamim explains that lest one think it is read as *sof* and means "end of the sea," Rashi is clarifying that it means a sea full of reeds. Despite the controversy among the commentators, it is clear that according to the Masoretic tradition, the word is read as *suf*. Any *ba'al koreh* will confirm this.

How was Yam Suf[7] understood in antiquity?[8] The Septuagint (second to third century BCE) translated Yam Suf into Greek as *Erythra Thalassa* or Red Sea—that is, neither "end" nor "reed!"[9] Thus, 2,200 years ago, long before the Bible was translated into Old English, the Septuagint identified the Yam Suf the Israelites crossed as the Red Sea. Josephus (*Antiquities* 2:15:3) identifies the Yam Suf as the Red Sea as well. This translation was carried over into the Latin when the fourth-century Latin Vulgate translated Yam Suf in Exodus 13:18 as *Mare Rubrum*, and in other places it translates Yam Suf as Mare Erythrae, both of which mean Red Sea.

Early English translations of the Bible, such as the 1611 *King James Version*, continued to translate Yam Suf as the Red Sea. Evidently, the theory that Red Sea is a corruption of the correct Old English (OE) translation, Reed (Rede) Sea, is unfounded.

Another important authoritative work maintains the tradition of identifying Yam Suf as Red Sea. In his commentary on the Bible, known as *Tafsir*, Rabbi Sa'adia Gaon (d. 942 CE), who lived in Egypt and Israel as well as in Baghdad, translated Yam Suf as *Bahr al Qulzum*, the Arabic name used for the Red Sea till this very day. Thus, it is clear that Jews at the time of the Geonim took

it for granted that the Yam Suf in the Bible refers to the modern-day Red Sea.[10]

Another fascinating piece of evidence comes from a tribe in India that claims to be descended from the Lost Tribe of Menashe. Author Hillel Halkin[11] cites evidence in support of this claim, such as a "Red Sea Song." The song contains many Biblical details regarding the Exodus: cloud by day, fire by night, water split in two, miraculous water from a rock, Divine delivery of quail, et cetera. It also calls the sea that was parted the Red Sea. While the exact age of the song is unknown, it is purported to be ancient.

The Hebrew word *suf* does not mean red literally. So where did the name "Red Sea" come from? There are various suggestions. Let's first look at the other places where Yam Suf is mentioned in the Bible and is translated as "Red Sea." In I Kings (9:26) it states that King Solomon based his navy on the Yam Suf near Eilat. This Yam Suf was probably not the one crossed by the Israelites[12] and may have been termed "red" after the inhabitants of the surrounding mountains, the people of Edom (see Genesis 25:30), which means red. Or the Sea might have been named so due to the reddish coral in the vicinity. (This is also probably why the country Eritrea is called so; Eritrea, whose name is a rendition of the ancient Greek name *Erythraía*, or the "Red Land," is located on the southwestern shore of the Red Sea.) Or it may be that the mineral-rich red mountain ranges and desert sands surrounding the sea inspired mariners of antiquity to name the sea *Mare Rostrum*, Red Sea. Rabbi Aryeh Kaplan (*The Living Torah*, Exodus 2:3, p. 260) suggests that the name Red Sea is based on the fact that in the language spoken in Ethiopia, *supho* denotes a red-topped kind of plant. Alternate possibilities (*The Living Torah*, Exodus 10:19, p. 304-5) include that its name derived from the ancient nation Erythria, so named because its inhabitants painted their faces red; or that it's based on the seasonal blooms of the red-colored *Trichodesmium erythraeum* near the water's

---

[7] It may even be possible to read it as *suf* and have it mean end. A similar word, such as in Esther 9:28 "*vezichram lo ya-suf mizaram*, nor the memory of them shall cease from their descendents," with *ya-suf* having a meaning akin to end.

[8] The most important ancient translator, from a Jewish perspective, is the first to second-century Onkelos. Unfortunately, he does not contribute to this discussion because he translates, or more accurately transliterates, Yam Suf as Yama Suf. However, the transliterated name is sometimes the most accurate "translation." For example, no one translates New York into Hebrew as "York Hachadasha" but rather as "New York."

[9] For references to the Red Sea, see also: 1 Maccabees 4:9; Wisdom of Solomon 10:18, 19:7 and Judith 5:12.

[10] I thank Rabbi Dr. Seth Mandel for the information in this paragraph.

[11] *Across the Sabbath River: In Search of a Lost Tribe of Israel* (New York, 2002), p. 222 and related notes on 377-378; p. 347 and related notes on 386-387.

[12] A recent theory proposes that the crossing did indeed take place at the Gulf of Aqaba; there are even claims of material evidence to prove this.

surface. The author of the column "Philologos," in the *Forward* (April 14, 2000, p. 12) suggests that the Gulf of Aqaba, which flows past ancient Edom and into Eilat, was once known as Yam Edom, which can mean the Sea of Edom or the Red Sea. He suggests that this name was eventually transferred, erroneously, to the other side of the Sinai, where it stuck.

Those who translate Yam Suf as Sea of Reeds do so because they prefer to translate it literally. But literal translations do not work all the time. This is especially true in this case since the precise definition of *suf* is unclear. Rashi (Exodus 2:3) identifies it as "*rosel*" in Old French (possibly "*roseau*" in modern French), which means a kind of flexible rhizome found along the edges of shallow, usually stagnant ponds. Like reeds, this is freshwater vegetation, which is not found at the edge of a salt sea such as the Red Sea. Rashi, based on *Sotah* 12b, finds a parallel in Isaiah 19:6, *kaneh vesuf ka'mailu*— the reeds and *suf* will dry up. From this verse it is clear that *suf* may be a plant that is similar to, but not synonymous with, *kaneh*, reed. Thus, Reed Sea is not even an accurate literal translation! Rashi elsewhere (*Sotah* 12b) identifies *suf* as a thin *aravah*, willow. Rabbi Kaplan suggests (*The Living Torah*, Exodus 2:3, p. 260) that *suf* is from *thuf*, the ancient Egyptian word for uncut papyrus. (Indeed the Latin translation of the Bible translates *suf* in Exodus 2:5 as papyrus.) He compares it to other places in Tanach (Exodus 2:3, 5) where *suf* seems to mean a type of reed (Isaiah 19:6; Jonah 2:6). Professor Yehuda Feliks (*Chai Vetzome'ach B'Torah*, 5744, p. 215) identifies the *suf* as the cattail or bulrush (genus *Typha*). This is not the same as *kaneh*, reed, which he identifies (*Hatzome'ach VeHa'Chai B'Mishnah*, 5743, p. 146) as being from the *Gramineae* (*Poaceae*, grasses) family and one of two species: *Arundo donax* (giant cane or giant reed) and *Phragmites communis* (*Phragmites australis*, the common reed).

The Exodus Route

This discussion also bears on what route the fleeing Israelites took. If Yam Suf is a sea with reeds, it rules out identifying it as either the Red Sea or the Mediterranean. The Red Sea is a long saltwater inlet separating the Arabian Peninsula from the east coast of Egypt. The sea with reeds would have to be freshwater, or at least

brackish, in order for reeds to flourish at its shore. This lends credence to the theory that Yam Suf was one of the shallow, marshy, bitter lakes east of the Nile Delta, such as a shallow spot connecting the Great and Little Bitter Lakes. Rabbi Kaplan (*The Living Torah*, Exodus 13:18, p. 321) cites sources that the Yam Suf was located at the mouth of the Nile, possibly identified with Lake Manzaleh. Other Biblical passages, in which Yam Suf refers to a body of water in a context other than the Exodus, indicate that its location was well known in Biblical times and that it was likely near Eilat and the Gulf of Aqaba, and not near the Bitter Lakes region of the Nile Delta (e.g., Exodus 23:31; Numbers 21:4; Deuteronomy 2:1; Judges 11:17-17; I Kings 9:26; and Jeremiah 49:21).

Three basic routes for the Exodus have been proposed by modern scholars who reject the Red Sea theory. Some propose a northern route whereby the Israelites went north to the coast and then eastward, and the "sea" they crossed was part of Lake Sirbonis, an arm or bay of the Mediterranean, and they then turned south into the Sinai Peninsula. Others, suggesting a central route, claim that the body of water crossed was a shallow lake north of the Red Sea called the Reed Sea. Indeed some of the lakes north of the Red Sea are abundant with reed-like plants. Finally, there are those who suggest a southern route and translate Yam Suf as the "sea at the end of the world."[13] Da'at Mikra (Shemot 13:18) finds support for his claim that the body of water crossed was at the northern end of the Gulf of Suez from Isaiah 11:15, which speaks about the "tongue of the Sea of Egypt."

Place names in the Bible, particularly those that sound similar or seem to refer to an equivalent location, can cause further confusion. Is the location called simply Suf (Deuteronomy 1:1) identical to Yam Suf, as many suggest? Might Sufa (Numbers 21:14) be the name of a place, even Yam Suf?

In other Biblical references, Yam Suf unequivocally refers to what is today called the Red Sea or its arms, the Gulf of Suez and Gulf of Aqaba. In I Kings 9:26 it states: "King Solomon also built a fleet of ships at Ezion

---

[13] See Bernard F. Batto, "Red Sea or Reed Sea," *Biblical Archaeology Review* (July-August 1984): 57-63, who argues that the correct pronunciation is Yam Sof and the meaning is the "distant, southern sea, at the end of the land."

Geber, which is near Eilat on the shore of the Red Sea [Yam Suf], in the land of Edom." If this were a marshy lake close to Egypt, this would certainly be a strange place for King Solomon to build his great fleet. The assumption is that the Eilat in Kings is the port at the northernmost end of the Gulf of Aqaba, the same location of modern-day Eilat.

Another reference indicating that it is the modern Red Sea is the list of encampments of the Israelites in the desert, as found in Numbers 33: 8-10. The Torah states that after the Israelites crossed "the Yam,"[14] they camped in Marah, then Elim and then "they camped by the Yam Suf." How could they have crossed the Sea of Reeds and, after many days of travel, still camped by that same Sea of Reeds? No body of water in the region except the Red Sea is large enough for them to have traveled for so long and still be close to its coast. Other references that support the identification of Yam Suf with Red Sea are Numbers 21:4, Deuteronomy 1:40, 2:1 and Jeremiah 49:21.

It is likely that the name Yam Suf and/or Red Sea was applied in the ancient world to more than one location. Professor Nahum M. Sarna (*Exploring Exodus* [New York, 1986], 106-110) says that Yam Suf is used in the Torah to refer to both the Gulf of Suez (between Egypt and the Sinai) and the Gulf of Aqaba (between the Sinai and Saudi Arabia). This is also supported by one of the Dead Sea Scrolls, known as the Genesis Apocryphon.[15] In a section of this Aramaic text (1Q20, column 21, lines 17-18; see Michael Wise, trans., *Dead Sea Scrolls Reader*, Brill ed., vol. 3, p. 31) Abraham describes his travels up the Gichon River, to the Mediterranean and beyond. He states, ". . . until I came to the Euphrates River. I journeyed along the Euphrates until I reached the Red Sea in the east, whence I followed the coast of the Red Sea until I came to the tongue of the Yam Suf, jutting out from the Red Sea." This indicates that the Red Sea branches off of Yam Suf. A tributary can easily be called after the main

body; thus, it would not be strange to identify the Yam Suf as the Red Sea. In recounting the story of Genesis, Josephus (*Antiquities* I:1:39) says that the Euphrates and Tigris end in the Erythraean Sea, literally the Red Sea.

In summary, Yam Suf in the Bible refers to multiple places, many of which were translated by the ancients as Red Sea. Similarly, specific bodies of water were referred to by multiple names, such as the Mediterranean Sea, which seems to have at least three names: Yam Plishtim (Exodus 23:32), Yam Hagadol (Numbers 34:6, 7) and Yam Ha'acharon (Deuteronomy 34:2). This leaves a translator in a serious quandary. But it is important to remember that translations are not always meant to be literal but rather to inform the reader of the target language what was intended in the source language.

Thus, in general, Yam Hagadol is translated in English as Mediterranean Sea and not as Great Sea; Moshe is called Moses and not "drawn forth," Yam Hamelach is referred to as Dead Sea and not as Salt Sea,[16] and Sha'ar Ha'ashpot is translated as Dung Gate and not Refuse Gate.

Thus, it is possible that the name Yam Suf has nothing to do with *suf* and was simply the name of the body of water.[17] The name need not have any meaning beyond that, similar to other names of locations (there are not and have never been buffalo in Buffalo, New York, and Beit Lechem, a hilly region, is not known for either its bread or its wheat).

While no one today can state definitively which body of water God split so that the Israelites could pass, the most ancient translations translate Yam Suf in the Exodus story as Red Sea. I would argue that despite the fact that reeds cannot grow in the Red Sea, we should accept the tradition of the Septuagint and of the Geonim and

---

[14] The body of water crossed is also referred to simply as *ha'yam* in Exodus 14:9, 21, 22.

[15] See N. Avigad and Y. Yadin, *A Genesis Apocryphon* (Jerusalem, 1956); Maurice Copisarow, "The Ancient Egyptian, Greek, and Hebrew Concept of the Red Sea," *Vetus Testamentum* XII (1962); Joseph A. Fitzmyer, *The Genesis Apocryphon of Qumran Cave I: A Commentary* (Rome, 1966); and Eliezer Segal, "Red Sea, Reed Sea…and the Persian Gulf," (Jewish Free Press, March 1991, also at http://people.calgary.ca/~elsegal/Shokel/9 10329_Red_Sea.html).

[16] One has to credit ArtScroll for being consistent in its policy of translating places literally. It translates Yam Hamelach as Salt Sea (Genesis 14:3, Numbers 34:2 and 34:12) and Yam Hagadol as Great Sea (Numbers 34:6, 7). In truth, while the Yam Suf translation may be justifiable because of the ArtScroll policy of translating according to Rashi, the other two translations cited are inexplicable. Even ArtScroll does not translate Abraham's two sons as "He is rejoicing" and "May God listen."

[17] This is, in fact, the subject of a Tannaic dispute. In the context of the infant Moshe story, Rabbi Shmuel bar Nachmani says that *suf* refers to a marsh with reeds and willows. But Rabbi Elazar opines that *suf* was shorthand for Yam Suf, and the Torah was not describing the physical surroundings but the actual location (*Shemot Rabbah* 1:21; *Sotah* 12a-b).

translate Yam Suf as the Red Sea. For those who cannot tolerate anything but a literal translation, they can always simply refer to Yam Suf as the Cattail Sea.

Jewish Action 70, no. 3 (2010):62-65
Reprinted with permission of *Jewish Action*, the magazine of the Orthodox Union

What's the Truth about ... the Meaning of "Pesach"?

by **Rabbi Dr. Ari Zivotofsky**

Misconception: The only meaning of "Pesach," the Hebrew name for the holiday of Passover, is "to pass over."

Fact: While that is a correct translation, an equally valid, and possibly older, translation is "to have compassion for."[18]

Background: The name of the spring holiday, and its associated temple animal offering, is based on a description first found in Exodus 12:12-13, where God declares, "And I shall pass through the land of Egypt on that night [of Passover], and I shall smite every firstborn in the land of Egypt from human to animal . . . and I will see the blood [on the doorposts], *ufasachti* you. . . . " The root *peh-samach-chet* is commonly translated as "and I will pass over." In this verse, the word *fasachti* indicates that God will "pass over" the Jewish houses in Egypt. However, it is a rare word in the Bible, and its translation is uncertain.

In his Aramaic translation of that verse, Onkelos (circa first century CE) uses the word *"ve'eychos,"* which

means "I will have compassion." Another early translator, Targum (pseudo-)Yonatan, also translates the word in a number of places as "having mercy" (Exodus 12:13; 12:17). But in 12:23 he translates *ufasach* as *veyagin*—to protect.

The Septuagint offers both definitions. In Exodus 12:23 it uses the classical translation of "to pass over," while in Exodus 12:13 and 12:27, it uses the word for shelter/protection.

The Mechilta records a dispute between Rebbi Yoshiya and Rebbi Yonatan over the word *pasachti*. Rebbi Yoshiya links it to *"pasaiti,"*[19] I stepped over, and explains that it means that God "skipped or passed over" the Jewish homes.[20] (This notion of God "skipping along" to expedite redemption,[21] he tells us, is found in a verse in Song of Songs (2:8): "The voice of my beloved, it comes suddenly to redeem me, as if skipping over the hills.") Rebbi Yonatan disagrees and explains that *pasachti* means that God had mercy on the Jews. Mechilta d'Rebbi Yishmael expresses this thought as well that *"Ein pischa ela chayis"*—"There is no [translation of] pesach other than mercy."

Rav Saadya Gaon[22] explains *"pasach"* (Exodus 12:23) as *veyerachem*, to have mercy, and *"zevach pesach"* (Exodus 12:27) as *"zevach chamlah,"* the sacrifice of mercy. Similarly, the Hebrew grammarian Ibn Janach,[23] in his *Sefer HaShorashim*, understands the word *pasach* as "to derive from mercy or grace."

Rashi quotes both opinions. Commenting on Exodus 12:13, he first compares *ufasachti* to a word with the same root[24] in Isaiah 31:5 and defines it as "to have

---

[18] Two sources that discuss some of this material are Raphael Weiss, "Pesachchamal, Chos" [Hebrew], L'shonainu (5723-5724): 27-28, 127-130 and S.P. Brock, "An Early Interpretation of Pasah: 'Aggen in the Palestinian Targum," Interpreting the Hebrew Bible: Essays in Honour of EIJ Rosenthal, ed. JA Emerton and Stefan C. Reif (Cambridge,1982), 27-34.

[19] Interchanging a *chet* and an *ayin* is not uncommon, as noted by Ramban to Deuteronomy 2:23, where he posits that *"eivim"* and *"cheivim"* are the same.

[20] Both Josephus (Antiquities 2:313) and Philo also understood it to mean "pass over." See Louis H. Feldman, *Translation of Josephus, Antiquities*, Book 2, p. 222, note 823.

[21] See also *Oznayim LaTorah* to Exodus 12:11.

[22] Lived 882-942. See *Encyclopaedia Judaica* 14:543-555.

[23] Lived in the first half of the eleventh century. See *EJ* 8:1181-1186.

[24] It is worth noting that the root *peh-samach-chet* has another meaning in Arabic, and possibly did in Aramaic as well. It means, "to clear an area." Thus, the statement in *Ha Lachma Anya: kol ditzrich yaitay v'yifsach*—is usually understood to mean that all should partake of the *Korban Pesach*. This presents a problem because the *Korban* is supposed to be eaten only *limnuyav*—to those

compassion." He then compares it to I Kings 18:21 and says that it means "to skip over."[25] Rashi prefers the second alternative, and on Exodus 12:11 cites only that translation. Interestingly, Rashi's biological and spiritual descendant, Rashbam, drops the other definition and offers only to "skip over" and to "pass by."

Those who reject "pass over" as the translation may be motivated by an aversion to ascribing physical characteristics to God, and, in particular, what Rambam calls "po'alei tenu'ah," action verbs. Onkelos consistently reinterprets anything that even resembles anthropomorphizing God. He would rather ascribe an emotion, such as mercy, to God than suggest that God physically skipped over houses.

There is, however, an intriguing suggestion[26] concerning this enigmatic word. If, as stated emphatically in the Haggadah and in Exodus 12:13, God himself killed all the Egyptian firstborn sons, then pasachti refers to God, so to speak, skipping over the Jewish houses. However, according to another verse in Exodus (12:23), it appears that the Angel of Death, not God, carried out the killing of the firstborns. In 12:23, the Bible states that God "ufasach the entrance and He will not permit the destroyer to enter your homes...."[27] Based on the literal reading of this verse, ufasach cannot mean God "passed over" the houses, since He wasn't doing the destroying; it must mean that God had mercy and protected the Jews from the Angel of Death.

The common notion that pesach means "pass over" is probably because the commentator par excellence, Rashi, inclined towards that approach. It is also possible

that our conception of the word was influenced by non-Jewish society. St. Jerome, in his fourth-century Vulgate, translated Exodus 12:13 as, "I will see the blood and I will pass over (ac transibo) you," and this passed into the overwhelming majority of Christian translations, including the English King James Bible.

There are a number of ramifications to the debate over the translation of the root peh-samach-chet. The discussion in the Mechilta, as explained by Malbim, is more than just a debate over translation; it is a debate over who was killed during the Plague of the Firstborn. Rav Yoshiya maintained that God, as the destroyer, "passed" or "skipped" over the Jewish homes and did not enter them at all. If an Egyptian was resourceful enough to hide out with a Jew, Rav Yoshiya believes that he was spared. Rav Yonatan, however, believes that God had mercy on the Jews, wherever they were, and only on the Jews. Thus, an Egyptian in a Jewish house was killed, and a Jew in an Egyptian house was spared.

This debate also has ramifications for every Jew at the Seder table. The Haggadah cites a Talmudic statement of Rabban Gamliel (Pesachim 116a-b) that whoever neglects to mention [Korban] Pesach, matzah and marror and fails to explain[28] the reason for their appearance at the Seder has not fulfilled his obligation.[29] He also states that one is required to explain to the assembled that the [Korban] Pesach is because God pasach over our ancestors' homes in Egypt as the verse (Exodus 12:27) states: "And you shall say, 'It is a Pesach sacrifice to Hashem who pasach the houses of the Israelites.'" It thus seems that in order to fulfill one's obligation, one is required to properly translate the word "pasach." (In this vein, some of the Haggadah commentators try to help out. For example, the Perush Kadmon, an anonymous, early commentary, written around the twelfth century, explains, based on I Kings 18:21 and Isaiah 31:5, that it means to pass over and not dwell on a spot.[30] The

---

pre-registered. With the alternate meaning the phrase can be understood as, "Come, clear a space, sit and eat," with no mention of the Korban Pesach.

[25] On this verse Radak and Metzudat Tzion say it means alternating or skipping between possibilities, as a cripple hobbles from side to side. Commenting on I Kings 18:26 (the verse that Chizkuni to Exodus 12:13 uses as his proof text that it means to step over), Metzudat Tzion, Metzudat David and Rashi all offer only one possibility, that it means to skip or to step over.

[26] Offered by my friend Shimon Gesundheit in his Ph.D. dissertation (Hebrew University).

[27] Note the use of the word pesach ("pass over" or "had mercy") in conjunction with pesach (entrance way). The words, of course, sound the same, assuming one uses the Ashkenazic pronunciation. A humorous example where Ashkenazic pronunciation has led to a comic error occurs in Zevachim 115a, Rashi s.v. yachol she'ani, where the word pesach in the verse "to the entrance (petach/pesach) of the Ohel Moed" is written with a samach instead of a taf.

[28] See for example Rashbam, Pesachim 116b; Meiri, Pesachim 116a; Tosafot Yom Tov on the mishnah; the Abudraham on the Haggadah and Chayei Adam 129:11 that it is not sufficient to merely mention the three items. The explanation of their appearance must also be provided.

[29] Whether Rabban Gamliel was referring to the obligation to recite the Haggadah or to eat the requisite items is hotly debated by the commentators on the Talmud and the Haggadah. This statement is cited as the halachah (Rambam, Chametz Umatzah 7:5).

[30] Similar to Rebbi Yoshiya in the Mechilta.

Shibbolei Haleket[31] similarly endorses the "skip over" translation based on the verse in I Kings. Rashbatz,[32] while also explaining it to mean "pass over," rejects the notion that *pasach* means "to rest," an explanation that must have been current in his time but is not readily found in other sources.)

Irrespective of what the root *peh-samach-chet* means, that night in Egypt revealed both God's mercy and the bypassing of Jews from destruction. How to precisely translate the Biblical term "*pasach*" is unclear and was already subject to debate more than 2,000 years ago. It seems that towards the medieval period the translation of "pass over" gained in prominence. That, however, does not negate the alternative possibility; and an opinion found in the Mechilta, Onkelos, Rav Saadya Gaon and other important sources should be accorded appropriate respect. At the Seder, both options should be raised, and Biblical verses with this root should be explored.

Jewish Action 64, no. 3 (2004)
Reprinted with permission of *Jewish Action*, the magazine of the Orthodox Union

---

[31] Born approximately 1220 (4980).

[32] Rav Shimon ben Tzemach Duran 1361-1444.

Lesson 2

Taking a Bite Out of Life
Kosher Food Facts

Introduction

This week you'll learn about food fit for a feast—a kosher feast, that is. Why is roasted cow udder like a tofu-cheese burger? Why do Jews love gefilte fish? Who invented glatt kosher? Finally, which is more likely to be served one day at a bar mitzvah: green eggs and ham or roasted giraffe?

Some say this lesson will enhance your health; others assert it will make you more of a *mensch*; still others argue it will benefit your soul. Study it and decide for yourself.

I. The Kosher Signs

A. Divine Imitations

Learning Interaction 1

"Kosher food"—what does that mean?

a. **Food blessed by a rabbi**

b. **A Jewish ethnic cuisine**

c. **Food produced under rabbinical supervision**

d. **Food that adheres to the many dos and don'ts of Jewish law**

e. **Food without bacon or shellfish**

Text 1

וַיְדַבֵּר ה' אֶל מֹשֶׁה וְאֶל אַהֲרֹן לֵאמֹר אֲלֵהֶם.
דַּבְּרוּ אֶל בְּנֵי יִשְׂרָאֵל לֵאמֹר זֹאת הַחַיָּה אֲשֶׁר תֹּאכְלוּ מִכָּל הַבְּהֵמָה אֲשֶׁר עַל הָאָרֶץ. כֹּל
מַפְרֶסֶת פַּרְסָה וְשֹׁסַעַת שֶׁסַע פְּרָסֹת מַעֲלַת גֵּרָה בַּבְּהֵמָה אֹתָהּ תֹּאכֵלוּ.
אַךְ אֶת זֶה לֹא תֹאכְלוּ מִמַּעֲלֵי הַגֵּרָה וּמִמַּפְרִיסֵי הַפַּרְסָה אֶת הַגָּמָל כִּי מַעֲלֵה גֵרָה הוּא
וּפַרְסָה אֵינֶנּוּ מַפְרִיס טָמֵא הוּא לָכֶם. וְאֶת הַשָּׁפָן כִּי מַעֲלֵה גֵרָה הוּא וּפַרְסָה לֹא יַפְרִיס
טָמֵא הוּא לָכֶם. וְאֶת הָאַרְנֶבֶת כִּי מַעֲלַת גֵּרָה הִוא וּפַרְסָה לֹא הִפְרִיסָה טְמֵאָה הִוא
לָכֶם. וְאֶת הַחֲזִיר כִּי מַפְרִיס פַּרְסָה הוּא וְשֹׁסַע שֶׁסַע פַּרְסָה וְהוּא גֵּרָה לֹא יִגָּר
טָמֵא הוּא לָכֶם . . .
אֶת זֶה תֹּאכְלוּ מִכֹּל אֲשֶׁר בַּמָּיִם כֹּל אֲשֶׁר לוֹ סְנַפִּיר וְקַשְׂקֶשֶׂת בַּמַּיִם בַּיַּמִּים וּבַנְּחָלִים
אֹתָם תֹּאכֵלוּ. וְכֹל אֲשֶׁר אֵין לוֹ סְנַפִּיר וְקַשְׂקֶשֶׂת בַּיַּמִּים וּבַנְּחָלִים מִכֹּל שֶׁרֶץ הַמַּיִם וּמִכֹּל
נֶפֶשׁ הַחַיָּה אֲשֶׁר בַּמָּיִם שֶׁקֶץ הֵם לָכֶם.
ויקרא יא,א–י

God spoke to Moses and Aaron, telling them to speak to the Israelites, and convey the following to them:

Of all the animals in the world, these are the ones that you may eat: Among mammals, you may eat [any one] that has true hooves that are cloven and that brings up its cud.

However, among the cud-chewing, hoofed animals, these are the ones that you may not eat:

The camel shall be unclean to you although it brings up its cud, because it does not have a true hoof.

The hyrax shall be unclean to you although it brings up its cud, because it does not have a true hoof.

The hare shall be unclean to you although it brings up its cud, because it does not have a true hoof.

The pig shall be unclean to you although it has a true hoof that is cloven, because it does not chew its cud. . . .

This is what you may eat of all that is in the water: You may eat any creature that lives in the water, whether in seas or rivers, as long as it has fins and scales. All creatures in seas and rivers that do not have fins and scales, whether they are small aquatic animals or other aquatic creatures, must be avoided by you.

Leviticus 11:1–10

Question for Discussion

In your estimation, does eating kosher imitations of non-kosher foods violate the spirit of the laws of kosher?

Text 2

אמרה ליה ילתא לרב נחמן, "מכדי כל דאסר לן רחמנא שרא לן כוותיה.

אסר לן דמא, שרא לן כבדא . . .

חלב בהמה, חלב חיה; חזיר, מוחא דשיבוטא . . .

בעינן למיכל בשרא בחלבא".

אמר להו רב נחמן לטבחי, "זויקו לה כחלי".

תלמוד בבלי, חולין קט,ב

Babylonian Talmud. A literary work of monumental proportions that draws upon the legal, spiritual, intellectual, ethical, and historical traditions of Judaism. The 37 tractates of the Babylonian Talmud contain the teachings of the Jewish sages from the period after the destruction of the 2nd Temple through the 5th century CE. It has served as the primary vehicle for the transmission of the Oral Law and the education of Jews over the centuries; it is the entry point for all subsequent legal, ethical, and theological Jewish scholarship.

Yalta said to [her husband] Rav Nachman: "It has been established that for everything that God forbade to us, He has permitted something similar.

"He forbade blood, but He permitted liver. . . .

"[He forbade certain] fats of domesticated animals, [but He permitted those same] fats of undomesticated animals.

"[He forbade] swine, [but He permitted] the brain of the *shibuta* fish. . . .

"Now I would like to eat [something that tastes like] milk and meat!"

Rav Nachman instructed his chefs, "Prepare for her an udder on a spit."

Talmud, Chulin 109b

Question for Discussion

Why would God intentionally create a permitted substitute for everything that He forbade?

Text 3

שלא יאמר אדם "אי איפשי ללבוש שעטנז אי אפשי לאכול בשר חזיר, אי איפשי לבוא על הערוה", אבל "איפשי מה אעשה ואבי שבשמים גזר עלי".

ספרא, קדושים, פרשה י

One should not say, "I have no desire to wear *shatnez*, to eat the flesh of the pig, to have illicit sex." Rather one should say, "I desire it; but I may not act on these desires, because my Father in heaven forbade it."

Midrash, Sifra, Parashat Kedoshim 10

Sifra. Also known as *Torat Kohanim.* A *tannaic* exegesis on the Book of Leviticus. The subject is predominately Temple-era related laws, inasmuch as the Book of Leviticus focuses primarily on the Temple service. The work is quoted often in the Talmud. According to Maimonides, the compiler and editor of this work was Rav (175–247 CE), a first generation Babylonian *amora*. Others attribute it to an earlier redactor.

Question for Discussion

What is the logic behind this statement?

B. The Quintessential Non-Kosher Animal

Text 4

II Maccabees is an apocryphal work originally written in Greek and is an abridgement of a longer work of five books by Jason of Cyrene, which is no longer extant. Its Greek title means "the narratives about Judah called the Maccabee." It tells about the corruptions of Hellenist priests and the deeds of Judah Maccabee.

Eleazar, one of the principal scribes, an aged man, and of a well-favored countenance, was constrained to open his mouth and to eat swine's flesh. But he, choosing rather to die gloriously, than to live stained with such an abomination, spit it forth.

II Maccabees, ch. 6

Question for Discussion

Why have antisemites chosen to humiliate the Jew specifically with the pig?

Text 5

Rabbi Shlomo Yitschaki (Rashi, 1040–1105). Most noted biblical and Talmudic commentator. Born in Troyes, France, Rashi studied in the famed *yeshivot* of Mainz and Worms. His commentaries on the Pentateuch and the Talmud, which focus on the simple understanding of the text, are considered the most fundamental of all the commentaries that preceded and followed. Since their initial printings, the commentaries have appeared in virtually every edition of the Talmud and Bible. Many of the famed authors of the *Tosafot* are among Rashi's descendants.

החזיר הזה כשהוא שוכב פושט טלפיו לומר, "ראו שאני טהור!"
רש"י, בראשית כו,לד

When the pig lies down, it extends its hooves, as if to say, "See, I am kosher!"

Rashi, Genesis 26:34

C. Kosher Pig

Text 6

וכבר ידעת מה שדרשו רבותינו ז"ל: למה נקרא שמו חזיר? שעתיד הקדוש ברוך הוא
להחזירו אלינו.

ריקאנטי, ויקרא יא,ב

Know what our sages have said: "Why is the pig
called a *chazir*? Because in the future, it will be
returned to the Jewish people."

Rabbi Menachem Rikanti, Leviticus 11:2

Rabbi Menachem Rikanti (ca. 1250–1310). Kabbalist, halachist, and author. Rabbi Rikanti was born in Italy. He wrote a Kabbalistic commentary on the Torah, a commentary on the prayer book, and a work dedicated to the 613 commandments. His halachic rulings were collected in *Piskei Rikanti* and were first published in Bologna in 1538.

II. Kosher = Healthy?

Learning Interaction 2

Indicate which of the following statements are true (T) and which are false (F):

T/F   It is proper to endeavor to understand the logic of God's commandments.

T/F   The purpose of the kosher laws is to safeguard physical health.

T/F   The purpose of the kosher laws is to protect the integrity of a person's intelligence, character, and behavior.

T/F   The purpose of the laws of kashrut is to instill within a person discipline and a sense of priorities.

T/F   Kosher eating has health benefits.

אַף עַל פִּי שֶׁכָּל חוֹקֵי הַתּוֹרָה גְּזֵרוֹת הֵם . . . רָאוּי לְהִתְבּוֹנֵן בָּהֶן וְכָל מַה שֶׁאַתָּה יָכוֹל לִיתֵּן לוֹ טַעַם תֵּן לוֹ טַעַם, הֲרֵי אָמְרוּ חֲכָמִים הָרִאשׁוֹנִים שֶׁהַמֶּלֶךְ שְׁלֹמֹה הֵבִין רוֹב הַטְּעָמִים שֶׁל כָּל חוֹקֵי הַתּוֹרָה.

משנה תורה, הלכות תמורה ד,יג

Rabbi Moshe ben Maimon (Maimonides/Rambam, 1135–1204). Halachic authority, philosopher, author, and physician. Maimonides was born in Cordoba, Spain. After the conquest of Cordoba by the Almohads, he fled Spain and eventually settled in Cairo, Egypt. There, he became the leader of the Jewish community and served as court physician to the vizier of Egypt. He is most noted for authoring the *Mishneh Torah*, an encyclopedic arrangement of Jewish law, and for his philosophical work, *Guide for the Perplexed*. His rulings on Jewish law are considered integral to the formation of halachic consensus.

Although all of the statutes of the Torah are decrees . . . it is fit to meditate upon them and wherever it is possible to provide a reason, one should provide a reason. The sages of the Talmud said that King Solomon understood most of the rationales for the statutes of the Torah.

Maimonides, *Mishneh Torah*, Laws of *Temurah* 4:13

Learning Interaction 3

Together with a partner, read Texts 8a and 8b, and answer the question that follows each text.

Text 8a

שהגוף כלי לנפש, ובו תעשה פעולתה, וזולתו לא תשלם מלאכתה לעולם . . . בהיות
בגוף שום הפסד מאי זה ענין שיהיה, תתבטל פעולת השכל כפי אותו הפסד. ועל
כן הרחיקתנו תורתנו השלמה מכל דבר הגורם בו הפסד. ועל הדרך הזה לפי הפשט
נאמר שבא לנו האיסור בתורה בכל מאכלות האסורות.
ואם יש מהם שאין נודע לנו ולא לחכמי הרפואה נזקן, אל תתמה עליהן, כי הרופא
הנאמן שהזהירנו בהן חכם יותר ממך ומהם. וכמה נסכל ונבהל מי שחשב שאין
לדברים נזק או תועלת אלא במה שהשיג הוא.

ספר החינוך, מצוה עג

Sefer Hachinuch is a work on the 613 commandments, arranged in the order of each *mitzvah's* appearance in the Torah. Four aspects of every mitzvah are discussed in this work: the definition of the mitzvah and its sources in the Written and Oral Torah; ethical lessons that can be deduced from the mitzvah; basic laws pertaining to the observance of the mitzvah; and who is obligated to perform the mitzvah and when. The work was composed in the 13th century CE by an anonymous author who refers to himself in the introduction as "the Levite of Barcelona." It has been widely thought that this referred to Rabbi Aharon Halevi of Barcelona (Re'ah); however, this view has been contested.

The body is an instrument of the soul: with it, the soul can carry out its activity; without it, it can never complete its work. . . . If there is any loss or damage in the body, of any kind, some function of intelligence will be nullified, corresponding to that defect. For this reason, our Torah sets a distance between us and anything that could be harmful. This explains in the most basic sense the Torah's prohibition against forbidden foods.

Even if there were among them foods whose danger is not known to us or to the wise physicians, we should not be astonished, for the Faithful Healer who has adjured us about them is wiser than you and they. How foolish and hasty would anyone be who thought that nothing is harmful or useful except as he understands it!

Sefer Hachinuch, Mitzvah 73

According to Text 8a, which of the following is true?

a. **The physical nature of non-kosher food is damaging to one's physical body.**

b. **The physical nature of non-kosher food is only damaging to one's mind, character, and behavior.**

c. **A metaphysical or spiritual entity within non-kosher food is damaging to one's spiritual identify.**

Text 8b 📜

והראוי שנדע, כי לא לענין בריאות הגוף וחליו, נאסרו אלו המאכלות, כמו שכתבו
קצת, חלילה, שאם כן נתמעטה מדרגת התורה האלהית מזה, מהיותה במדרגת חבור
קטן מספרי הרפואות הקצרים בדבריהם וטעמם, וזה מגונה.

מלבד שכבר איפשר לתקן אותם במיני תבולים או הרכבות, בהם יתבטל כח ההיזק
ההוא, כמו שמבטלין כח הסמים הממיתים, אשר מהם נעשו התרופות כלם, ואם כן
לא ישאר האיסור על עמדו, ותעשה התורה כפלסתר . . .

גם שהגוים הבלתי נשמרים, אוכלי בשר החזיר ושאר הבהמות והעופות והדגים
הטמאים, הנה ראינום שהם חיים על הבריאות, ואין עיף ואין כושל בהם לזאת הסבה.
אמנם מה שנאסרו להם, הוא לענין חולאי הנפש ובריאותה, כי הם מתועבים
ומשוקצים ומזיקים אל הנפש המשכלת, ומולידים בה האטימות ורוע המזג וקלקול
התאוות, אשר מהם תתהוה רוח הטומאה המטמא הדעות והמעשים, ומגרש רוח
הטהרה והקדושה ממנה.

עקידת יצחק, שער ס

Rabbi Yitschak Arma'ah (ca. 1420–1494) Philosopher, preacher, rabbi, and author. Rabbi Arma'ah served as rabbi of small Jewish communities in Aragon, and later, in Calatayud, Spain. To counteract the conversionist sermons Jews were compelled to attend, he delivered sermons of his own on the principles of Judaism, and these formed the basis of his later works. When Jews were expelled from Spain in 1492, he settled in Naples, Italy. He is best known for his work *Akeidat Yitschak*, a commentary on the Pentateuch.

Know that these foods were not forbidden to us because of their effect on our body's health, as some, sadly, have written. Were that so, it would have diminished the stature of the divine Torah, placing it at the level of those kinds of medical books that are short in their words and explanations. This would be disgraceful.

Besides, it would be possible to fix the harmful nature of these foods by adding various ingredients and admixtures that would nullify any damaging property, as we do with the deadly poisons that we transform into all kinds of healing medicines. Therefore, no prohibition should remain and the Torah would be like a fraud. . . .

Also we see that the non-Jews who are not careful about this and eat the meat of swine and other non-kosher animals, fowl, and fish, live in good health and show no weakness or infirmity on this account.

Rather, they are prohibited because of their effect on the soul and its health, for they are disgusting and repulsive, and damage the intellect, creating within it obstructions, an evil temperament, and a corruption of the desires. They bring about a spirit of impurity and contaminate one's character and one's actions, and they expel the spirit of purity.

Rabbi Yitschak Arma'ah, *Akeidat Yitschak, Sha'ar 60*

According to Text 8b, which of the following is true?

a.   The physical nature of non-kosher food is damaging to one's physical body.

b.   The physical nature of non-kosher food is only damaging to one's mind, character, and behavior.

c.   A metaphysical or spiritual entity within non-kosher food is damaging to one's spiritual identify.

Text 9 📜

ראוי לאדם להתבונן במשפטי התורה הקדושה, ולידע סוף ענינם כפי כחו. ודבר
שלא ימצא לו טעם ולא ידע לו עילה, אל יהי קל בעיניו . . . ולא תהא מחשבתו בו
כמחשבתו בשאר דברי החול . . .
הרי נאמר בתורה (ויקרא יט,לז) "ושמרתם את כל חקותי ואת כל משפטי ועשיתם
אותם" . . .
והמשפטים הן המצות שטעמן גלוי וטובת עשייתן בעולם הזה ידועה, כגון איסור גזל,
ושפיכות דמים, וכיבוד אב ואם.
והחוקים הן המצות שאין טעמן ידוע. אמרו חכמים, "חוקים חקתי לך ואין לך רשות
להרהר בהן" (יומא סז,א), ויצרו של אדם נוקפו בהן, ואומות העולם משיבין עליהן.
משנה תורה, הלכות מעילה ח,ח

I

t is appropriate for one to meditate on the laws of
the holy Torah to know their purpose according
to one's capacity. If one cannot find a reason or a
rationale for a practice, one should not regard it lightly.
. . . One's thoughts concerning them should not be like
his thoughts concerning other ordinary matters. . . .

The Torah states, (Leviticus 19:37): "And you shall
guard all My *chukim* and all My *mishpatim* and perform
them.". . . *Mishpatim* are *mitzvot* whose justifications are
revealed, and the practical benefits of their observance
are known: for example, the prohibitions against robbery
and bloodshed, and the commandment to honor one's
father and mother.

Chukim are *mitzvot* whose reasons are not known, as our sages said: "[God says,] 'I order you to observe My *chukim*, and you have no license to question them'" (Talmud, Yoma 67a). A person naturally chafes against their observance, and the nations of the world challenge them.

Maimonides, *Mishneh Torah*, Laws of Misappropriation of Sacred Property 8:8

Text 10

Christians, Muslims, Jews and Atheists alike are helping fuel the robust market for kosher foods, according to a new report by market research firm Mintel. In a consumer survey of adults who purchase kosher food, Mintel found that the number one reason people buy kosher is for food quality (62%).

The second most common reason people say they purchase kosher food is "general healthfulness" (51%) and the third is food safety (34%). This contrasts sharply to the just 14% of respondents who say they purchase kosher food because they follow kosher religious rules. Another 10% buy kosher because they follow some other religious rules with eating restrictions similar to kosher.

Mintel Press Release, February 2009

III. Understanding Names

A. Glatt Kosher

Learning Interaction 4

A glatt kosher product is:

a.   **any food produced under constant rabbinical supervision.**

b.   **any food produced by an Orthodox Jewish company.**

c.   **any food that meets a stricter set of kosher rules.**

d.   **any food that is both kosher and organic.**

e.   **none of the above.**

Text 11a

וְאַנְשֵׁי קֹדֶשׁ תִּהְיוּן לִי, וּבָשָׂר בַּשָּׂדֶה טְרֵפָה לֹא תֹאכֵלוּ, לַכֶּלֶב תַּשְׁלִכוּן אֹתוֹ.
שמות כב,ל

You shall be holy people unto Me; an animal that is mauled in the field you shall not eat; you shall throw it to the dogs.

Exodus 22:30

Question for Discussion

What is this verse forbidding?

Text 11b 📖

לֹא תַּחֲלוֹק בֵּין נוֹטָה לָמוּת בֵּין שֶׁטְּרָפָתָה חַיָּה וּשְׁבָרַתָּה, בֵּין שֶׁנָּפְלָה מִן הַגַּג וְנִשְׁתַּבְּרוּ
רוֹב צַלְעוֹתֶיהָ, בֵּין שֶׁנָּפְלָה וְנִתְרַסְּקוּ אֵיבָרֶיהָ, בֵּין שֶׁזָּרַק בָּהּ חֵץ וְנָקַב לִבָּהּ אוֹ רֵיאָתָהּ,
בֵּין שֶׁבָּא לָהּ חֹלִי מֵחֲמַת עַצְמָהּ וְנָקַב לִבָּהּ אוֹ רֵיאָתָהּ, אוֹ שִׁבֵּר רוֹב צַלְעוֹתֶיהָ, וְכַיּוֹצֵא
בָּהֶן, הוֹאִיל וְהִיא נוֹטָה לָמוּת מִכָּל מָקוֹם, הֲרֵי זוֹ טְרֵפָה . . .
אִם כֵּן לָמָּה נֶאֱמַר בַּתּוֹרָה "טְרֵפָה"? דִּבֶּר הַכָּתוּב בַּהֹוֶה.
שֶׁאִם לֹא תֹּאמַר כֵּן, לֹא תֵּאָסֵר אֶלָּא אוֹתָהּ שֶׁנִּטְרְפָה בַּשָּׂדֶה, אֲבָל אִם נִטְרְפָה בֶּחָצֵר
לֹא תֵּאָסֵר? הָא לָמַדְתָּ שֶׁאֵין הַכָּתוּב מְדַבֵּר אֶלָּא בַּהֹוֶה.

משנה תורה, הלכות מאכלות אסורות ד,ח

There is no difference between an animal that was attacked and battered by an animal, fell from the roof and broke the majority of its ribs, fell and crushed its limbs, was shot with an arrow that pierced its heart or lung, developed an illness that caused its heart or lung to be perforated, broke the majority of its ribs, or the like—because it is on the verge of death, regardless of the cause, it is a *tereifah*. . . .

If so, why does the Torah use the term *tereifah*? For the Torah speaks in terms of common situations.

Otherwise, we'd have to [arrive at the ludicrous conclusion] that only an animal that was mortally wounded in the *field* would be forbidden, and one that is mortally wounded in a courtyard would not be forbidden.

Maimonides, *Mishneh Torah*,
Laws of Forbidden Foods 4:8

Text **12a**

כל מקום שאסרו סרוכת הריאה, אין הפרש בין שתהא הסרכא דקה כחוט השערה בין שתהא עבה וחזקה ורחבה כגודל, ולא כאותם שממעכים ביד ואם נתמעכה תולין להקל.

שולחן ערוך, יורה דעה לט,י

Rabbi Yosef Caro (Beit Yosef/Maran, 1488–1575). Scholar, author, and Sefardic halachic authority. Beit Yosef and his family fled Spain after the edict of expulsion of 1492 and eventually settled in Safed, Israel. He authored a commentary called *Beit Yosef* on the halachic work, the *Arba'ah Turim*. His magnum opus, the *Shulchan Aruch* (Code of Jewish Law), has been universally accepted as the basis for modern Jewish law.

In all instances where an animal is rendered non-kosher due to an adhesion on the lung, it does not matter whether the adhesion is fragile and slight like a hair, or thick, sturdy, and wide like a thumb. While some massage the adhesion with their hands and permit the animal for consumption if it can be gently removed, this is not proper.

Rabbi Yosef Caro, *Shulchan Aruch, Yoreh De'ah*, 39:10

Glatt גלאט

Text 12b

וֵיֹש מַתִּירִין לְמַשְׁמֵשׁ בַּסְרָכוֹת וּלְמָעֵךְ בָּהֶם, וְאוֹמְרִים שֶׁסְּרָכָא אִם יְמַעֵךְ אָדָם בָּה בְּכָל
הַיּוֹם לֹא תִנָּתֵק. וְלָכֵן כָּל מָקוֹם שֶׁיִּתְמַעֵךְ תּוֹלִין לְהָקֵל, וְאוֹמְרִים שֶׁאֵינוּ סְרָכָא אֶלָּא רִיר
בְּעָלְמָא. וְאַף עַל פִּי שֶׁהוּא קוּלָא גְדוֹלָה, כְּבָר נָהֲגוּ כָּל בְּנֵי מְדִינוֹת אֵלּוּ, וְאֵין לִמְחוֹת
בְּיָדָם מֵאַחַר שֶׁיֵּשׁ לָהֶם עַל מַה שֶׁיִּסְמוֹכוּ.

רמ״א שם, לט,יג

There are those who permit the massaging and rubbing of the adhesions, for they maintain that a real adhesion [which would render an animal *tereifah*] would not dislodge even if massaged all day. Therefore, they are lenient with regard to any adhesion that can be rubbed off, saying that it is not a significant adhesion.

Even though this is a great leniency, those who do so should not be reprimanded, for this is the common practice in our entire region, and there is basis for their practice.

Rabbi Moshe Isserles, ibid., 39:13

Rabbi Moshe Isserles (Rema, 1525–1572). Scholar, author, and Ashkenazic halachic authority. Rema is the author of the *Mapah*, an explanatory commentary on the *Shulchan Aruch*, and *Darchei Moshe*, a commentary on the halachic compendium, *Arba'ah Turim*. As a youth, he studied in Lublin, later returning to Cracow where he was appointed rabbi. He is buried in the old Jewish cemetery in Cracow.

B. What Is Kosher Salt?

Text 13

וָאֹמַר לִבְנֵי יִשְׂרָאֵל, "דַּם כָּל בָּשָׂר לֹא תֹאכֵלוּ".

ויקרא יז,יד

And I say to the children of Israel, "You shall not eat the blood of any flesh."

Leviticus 17:14

Text 14

לא ימלח במלח דקה כקמח, ולא במלח גסה ביותר שנופלת מעל הבשר.

שולחן ערוך, יורה דעה סט,ג

One should not use salt that is fine like flour, nor salt that is exceedingly coarse that rolls off the meat.

Rabbi Yosef Caro, *Shulchan Aruch, Yoreh De'ah* 69:3

C. What Is Gefilte Fish?

Text 15

The Sabbath laws specify the preferred manner in which the edible part of the food shall be separated from the inedible portion, and even the manner in which the residue of the meal, such as the peelings and pits of fruit or the bones and skin of fish, can be removed from the table is laid down in the rules. To do so according to the strictures of *halakhah* requires a learning which not everyone possessed and which could not be expected from the indigent guests who were often invited to the Sabbath table. All of these problems were eliminated by serving the fish in boneless and skinless portions.

"Come and let us give credit to Israel, the holy people," writes a halakhic authority in the name of the Brisker Rav, "for establishing the custom of eating fish on the Sabbath in the form of stuffed fish, thereby eliminating all manner of religious scruples and doubts."

Eric G. Freudenstein, *Judaism* 29:4 (1980)

Eric G. Freudenstein, PhD (d. 2008). Scientist and scholar. Dr. Freudenstein left Germany as a young man with his family in 1936 and moved to England and then the United States. He was chief chemist for the giant kosher food firm Rokeach for 50 years. His articles on Jewish studies were collected and published in *Yad Gavriel*.

IV. Food Struggles

Text **16a**

Zohar. The seminal work of Kabbalah, Jewish mysticism. It is a mystical commentary on the Torah, written in Aramaic and Hebrew. According to Arizal, the Zohar consists of the teachings of Rabbi Shimon bar Yocha'i who lived in Israel during the 2nd century CE. The Zohar has become one of the indispensable texts of traditional Judaism, alongside and nearly equal in stature to the Mishnah and Talmud.

מאן דבעי לנהמא על פום חרבא ייכול.

זהר ג, קפח,ב

One who desires bread should eat it with the blade of a sword.

Zohar 3:188b

Text **16b**

שעת אכילה—שעת מלחמה.

זהר ג,רעב,א

The time of eating is a time of battle.

Zohar 3:272a

שהיה כח זה של עץ החיים ועץ הדעת טוב ורע בכל עצי הגן. ואם היה טועם מעץ
החיים, היינו שלא בהנאת הגוף, אז היה מרגיש בכל אכילתו מכל העץ שהיה אוכל
קדושת עץ החיים, והיינו אכילה בקדושה . . . אבל כיון שאכל מעץ הדעת, היינו
שהרגיש הנאת הגוף באכילה, על ידי זה נעשה ערבוב, וכל אכילות שאכל הרגיש
מעץ הדעת טוב ורע, הנאת הגוף.

פרי צדיק, פרשת בראשית ח

All the trees in the garden possessed the potential of both the Tree of Life and the Tree of Knowledge of Good and Evil. . . . Had Adam eaten from the Tree of Life—that is, had he eaten properly, and not merely to indulge his body—he would have experienced the holiness of the Tree of Life in his eating.

. . . But because he ate from the Tree of Knowledge, that is, with the awareness of his sensory pleasure, all subsequent eating was tainted with the desire for bodily gratification.

Rabbi Tsadok Hakohen Rabinowitz, *Peri Tsadik, Parashat Bereishit* 8

Rabbi Tsadok Hakohen Rabinowitz (1823–1900). Chasidic rebbe and prolific author. Born to a Lithuanian rabbinic family, as a young man he became a follower of Rabbi Mordechai Yosef Leiner of Izhbitsa. He authored many works on Jewish law, Chasidism, Kabbalah, and ethics, as well as scholarly essays on astronomy, geometry, and algebra. He is buried in Lublin.

Question for Discussion

How does this interpretation differ from the simple understanding of the biblical story?

Text 18 📖

"ואנשי קודש תהיון לי". ואמר הרבי מקוצק: כך אמר ה': "מלאכים ושרפים וחיות הקודש יש לי די מבלעדיכם, איני זקוק שתהיו לי מלאכים. אלא 'ואנשי קודש תהיון לי', שתהיו בני אדם ותחיו כבני אדם, וכבני אדם תהיו לי קדושים ואנשי קודש".

לתורה ולמועדים, שמות כה,ב

Rabbi Shlomo Yosef Zevin (1890–1978). Born in Kazimirov, Belarus; considered one of the eminent rabbis of the 20th century. A student of both the Lithuanian and Chasidic traditions, he was ordained by numerous prominent rabbis, including Rabbi Yosef Rosen of Rogatchov and Rabbi Yechiel Michel Epstein, author of *Aruch Hashulchan*. In 1934, he immigrated to Israel, where he resumed his life of scholarship. He was the chief editor of the *Talmudic Encyclopedia*.

"Y ou shall be holy people unto Me." The Rebbe of Kotsk said: This is what God is saying: "I have enough angels without you, I have no need for you to be angelic. Instead, 'you shall be holy *people* unto Me.' Be human, live as humans do—but be holy humans, a holy people.'"

Rabbi Shlomo Yosef Zevin, *LeTorah Ulemo'adim,* Exodus 25:2

Text 19 📖

והכוונה בכל זה לפסוק רוב התאוה והשלוח בבקשת הערב ולשום תאות המאכל ומשתה תכלית.

מורה הנבוכים ג,לה

The object of all these laws [concerning forbidden food] is to restrain the growth of desire, the indulgence in seeking that which is pleasant, and the disposition to consider the appetite for eating and drinking as the purpose of a person's existence.

Maimonides, *Guide for the Perplexed* 3:35

אסור לו לאדם שיהנה מן העולם הזה בלא ברכה . . . כל הנהנה מן העולם הזה בלא
ברכה, כאילו נהנה מקדשי שמים, וכתיב (תהלים כד,א), "לה׳ הארץ ומלואה".
תלמוד בבלי, ברכות לה,א

It is forbidden to enjoy anything of this world without reciting a blessing. . . . To enjoy anything of this world without a blessing is like making personal use of things consecrated to heaven, because it says, "The earth and all that is in it belongs to God" (Psalms 24:1).

Talmud, Berachot 35a

Lesson Summary

1. "Kosher" literally means "fit," or "appropriate." It refers to a set of Jewish dietary laws, comprised of many do's and don'ts that make food fit for consumption.

2. For an animal to be kosher, it must have cloven hoofs and chew its cud. For an aquatic creature to be kosher, it needs to have fins and scales.

3. For all foods that are not kosher to eat, there is a kosher equivalent that possesses a similar taste. According to the Talmud, there is nothing wrong with enjoying these foods.

4. God wants us to recognize that His intention in forbidding any given item is not in order to deprive us of the pleasure but for other important reasons.

5. For Jews, the pig has the distinction of being the quintessential non-kosher animal. One explanation for this is that Jews perceive the pig as being characterized by deceptiveness by the way it "capitalizes" on the fact that it has one of the signs that identify a kosher animal.

6. In life, we often encounter people or situations that are overtly unsavory or "non-kosher." We should be careful about evil that is cloaked in goodness because it is so much harder to overcome.

7. There is a Jewish tradition that the pig will become kosher when Moshiach arrives. Some understand this metaphorically; others explain it literally.

8. It is proper to endeavor to understand the logic of God's commandments, though we are aware that we may never grasp His ultimate reasoning.

9. Many people believe that kosher food is healthier than non-kosher foods. Some Jewish thinkers wrote that the laws of kashrut are to protect health. Others believed that it was to protect one's character and temperament. Kabbalah focuses on spiritual entities within non-kosher food that can be detrimental to the spiritual soul.

10. The kosher laws also remind us that eating and drinking is not the sole purpose of a person's existence.

11. God's commandments break down into two general categories: When we are able to understand and sense the rational, this mitzvah is a *mishpat*. When the understanding is beyond our perceivable experience, it is a *chok*.

12. *Treif*, or *tereifah*, in its narrowest sense, refers to an animal that was mauled by a predator and is mortally wounded. In Jewish law, any animal that is mortally wounded has the status of a *tereifah* and cannot be consumed, even if slaughtered properly.

13. Glatt kosher means that the lungs of an animal were checked and are free from any adhesions. Today, almost all kosher meat is *glatt*.

14. "Kosher salt," whose grains are coarser than average table salt, probably started off being called "koshering salt." To free meat from blood, Jewish law requires the use of coarse salt.

15. "Gefilte fish" is Yiddish for "stuffed fish." Jews would prepare such fish for Shabbat because it was more economical and because it would help avoid forbidden acts on Shabbat.

16. The Tree of Knowledge and the Tree of Life can be understood as two states of mind. The challenge of eating with holy consciousness is rooted in Adam and Chavah's eating from the Tree of Knowledge in the Garden of Eden.

17. Saying a blessing before we eat helps us eat with mindfulness. The blessing reminds us that everything was created by God and that we were created to fulfill His will.

Additional Readings

A Set of Dishes

by **Dr. Velvl Greene**

Even before we met Rabbi Moshe Feller in 1962 we would have been considered active and even committed Jews. Most of our friends were Jewish, our families were Jewish, our interests included Jewish "things," and our outlook was certainly Jewish. We read books published by the JPS, we listened to Jewish records, we treasured the Chagall prints in our home, and were dues-paying members of a Conservative synagogue. Gail was a leading soprano in the synagogue choir and I was one of the very few members who attended on most Friday nights, regardless of whose bar mitzvah was being celebrated that weekend. We were probably Zionists, too. We regularly contributed to the UJA, attended our city's Farband picnics, and were officers on the board of Herzl Camp.

Before we met Rabbi Feller, however, I don't remember doing anything deliberately, or for that matter, abstaining from anything deliberately, because and only because it was a Torah Commandment. Such thoughts never really entered my mind. One went to synagogue and lit candles and ate gefilte fish and wore a *tallit* (prayer shawl) because it was a traditional thing to do, and a pleasant tradition at that. Not to do so would be making a statement of denial, or of disinterest, or of apathy. I didn't care to deny or to be disinterested. It wasn't part of my self-image. On the other hand, we didn't keep kosher or refrain from driving on Shabbat, or any of those other things. They were simply not relevant. They played no role in my value system. Note that we were not consciously protesting or transgressing, as one hears about the early Jewish socialists or freethinkers having done. Those would be statements that we didn't care to make. We were, quite simply, "good American Jews" who didn't want to make waves. Of course, we knew that some Jews avoided non-kosher food and didn't drive on Shabbat. (There were remarkably few of them in our town, then.) And those were *their* traditions and *their*

choices. We didn't think they were wrong—only slightly behind on the social evolution scale.

Looking back at those simpler days, I think that our lives reflected the characteristic paradox of the modern secular Jew: interested in Jewish things but basically ignorant; active in Jewish circles but limited in choice; committed to community, family, profession and the "Jewish People" but quite unaware of the foundation that informs this commitment. And above all, quite devoid of the learning and experience which permit discrimination between significance and triviality, reality and fraud. There must have been thousands like me. There still are. You see them arriving in Israel by the busload in "young leadership groups" or "fact finding missions" or "synagogue tours." They are too busy raising funds to spend much time thinking; they are too involved with the present to research the past; they are too committed to the global picture to worry about the Jewish survival of their own children, or even themselves.

Actually, if we hadn't been in this kind of pattern ourselves, we probably wouldn't have met Rabbi Feller. He sought me out because I was a potentially rising star of the Jewish community. He was trying to organize his first banquet and wanted my name as well as others like me on his sponsors' committee.

The story of our first meeting has been told often enough (it was even mentioned in *Time* magazine) to obviate the need for retelling. On the surface it looked like a comedy. A strange, bearded, black-hatted young man remembers, just before sunset, that he has not yet said his afternoon prayers. Disregarding the fact that he is in my office, that he had asked for the appointment, that he is requesting a favor—he stands up, walks to the wall, ties a black cord around his waist and proceeds to mumble and shake. I will never forget my bewilderment and embarrassment. I didn't know what he was doing or why. I didn't know Jews prayed outside a synagogue. I didn't know they prayed in the afternoon. I didn't know they prayed on weekdays. And I didn't know how anyone could pray without someone announcing the page!

There were a lot of things I didn't know, then. But I did develop a definite interest and a special affection for this young man who was so pleasant and so different. He had a completely different set of rules to guide him—at once so radical and so archaic. He not only marched to the beat of a different drum—he seemed to enjoy the music more than we did ours. Above all, he was committed and consistent. I related to that. It is a beautiful trait in a world of laissez-faire religion and situation ethics.

In a short time we became friends—his family and ours. We discussed, we debated, we visited, we socialized. Gail and I were impressed with their sincerity and genuine warmth, but we still thought of them as anachronisms—as remnants of a past, as out of tune with the realities and needs of the modern American world. We didn't change our lifestyle because of them. Instead we kept waiting for them to change theirs. After all, nearly everyone else who had started out with a beard and hat ultimately did.

If he tried to influence us, during those early months, it must have been a very subtle effort. There was certainly no overt pressure or demand. Of course, they wouldn't eat at our house. But that wasn't a signal that something was wrong. They were so far out that their dietary idiosyncrasies were the least things one noticed. We started studying together, but our progress was infinitesimal. I asked too many questions, challenged too many axioms. I was definitely not a compliant student.

It could have gone on like this for a long time, if it weren't for our trip to Warsaw.

In the summer of 1963 I was invited to participate as a member of the American delegation in an international conference on space research in Poland. My balloon-borne samplers had discovered viable microorganisms in the stratosphere at a time when the field of exobiology was too full of speculation and embarrassingly lacking in real biological data. Whatever the real reasons for the invitation, it was an opportunity to be grabbed. In 1963, visits to Warsaw and Eastern Europe were very rare. Few

of my professional colleagues had been to Warsaw since the war. None of my Jewish friends, certainly.

Gail and I left the three children with my parents in Canada and we flew to Warsaw. It was a dismal visit. In those years the city had not yet recovered from the destruction of World War Two. Physical destruction was evident in the piles of rubble that covered huge sections of the city. The emotional destruction was worse. The indigenous Polish anti-Semitism which had been fueled generously by the German occupation was now being nurtured by the Jew-hatred of the new Russian masters. We were told that there were a few thousand lonely Jews left in Warsaw: a handful of Jewish Communists, some of whom we met in the office of the Yiddish newspaper; less than a handful of old men who attended services in the only synagogue left standing; several in the performing arts; and the rest who had returned from the camps after the war and didn't want to leave their dead and/or their memories. They had survived the war and now they were surviving the peace.

One evening we attended a performance in the Jewish Theater. It was an edited version of *Tevyeh the Milkman* in Yiddish. The only part of the script written by Sholem Aleichem that remained described the misery and pogroms of the Tzarist times. The rest of the play dealt with the promise of the coming Soviet revolution. The hero of the play was not even Tevyeh. As one can imagine, it was Tevyeh's son-in-law Feferl, the revolutionary who was exiled to Siberia. It made no difference. We were the only ones in the theater who listened to the performance. The rest of the audience was a tour group from Sweden who were listening to a simultaneous translation with earphones.

Even twenty years later, I still remember the chill (it was the middle of June) as we walked through the area where the ghetto had once stood. The walls and all the buildings had been leveled. Piles of stone and burned timbers still lay there. But one could see where the streetcar tracks had ended because a wall had once been built across them. And it was possible, with the aid of maps we had copied from Holocaust literature, to recognize the original street lines, and even their identities. We could find our way to the Umschlagge Platz, to Mila Street and to the old Jewish cemetery.

I remember crying at the tomb of I.L. Peretz, the great Jewish writer after whom the day school I attended in Winnipeg was named. I remember crying at the large mounds of earth that covered unmarked mass graves. I remember walking a lot and crying a lot. This, after all, was the Jewish heritage that I knew. There, but for the luck of somebody emigrating in time, was my home or my grave. This was the end of the Yiddishist, Socialist, Zionist, European Judaism I knew. I was affected more by Warsaw than I would be ten years later by the Yad Vashem Holocaust Memorial in Jerusalem. The latter is a more beautiful monument, tastefully done. It is a museum, a history lesson, a shrine, an antiseptic display. Warsaw was death and cultural annihilation.

Through it all, I wondered how Gail was being affected. After all, I was a product of the "Old Country" culture of Winnipeg. She came from the sterile culture of Southern California's Reform temples. Peretz and Sholem Asch and Warsaw were part of my upbringing. How was all of this moving her?

I found out on Saturday afternoon. We had visitors— a Polish Jew and his two children whom we had met at the cemetery and whom we invited for tea. We had heard that there was a Jewish school and wanted to hear more about it. He, it developed, was looking for a handout. The seven-year-old child knew nothing. The eleven-year-old proudly recited the sum total of his Jewish knowledge: the four questions from the Passover Haggadah. We drank tea. I gave them a gift and my business card, and they left. Then we both cried. The end of Warsaw's centuries of Jewish creativity was a little boy who could barely stammer out *"Mah Nishtanah."*

Then Gail reacted. She sat up on her bed where she had been crying and spoke the most firm words I had heard in our seven years of marriage:

"I don't know what you think and I don't really care, but I've made up my mind. As soon as we get back I'm going to ask Moishe to make our house kosher. We're the only ones left. There's no one else. If we lose it, if we don't do it, if our children don't know about it, there won't be any Jews anymore. You can do what you want. But our house is going to be Jewish."

It was a defiant proclamation and she meant it. The pictures, the books and the music were not enough. She intended to transform the house organically, its very essence. Moreover, she was as good as her word. When we arrived in Minneapolis, the first person she called was Rabbi Feller, and he was only too willing to comply.

I don't remember all of the details. But I do remember the shocked look on his face when he first looked into our refrigerator. To this sweet young man, fresh out of the *yeshiva,* non-kosher meant a scar on the pleura of the animal who supplied the meat; or one drop of milk in fifty drops of chicken soup. The sight of real pork and shellfish must have been shattering. But bit by bit he "put our house in order." He introduced us to a kosher butcher; he taught us to look for the kashrut emblem on packaged food; he spent hours boiling silverware and metal utensils; he supervised the blowtorching of our oven; Mrs. Feller helped Gail buy new dishes.

One item gave him trouble: an expensive set of English bone china which we had received as a wedding gift from my sisters in Canada. It was a beautiful set and without doubt, one of our more precious possessions. Gail was quite eager to "kasher" the dishes by soaking and heating. She wanted to use them for Shabbat. I'm sure the whole project would have ended if she had been told then that the only way to kasher china, even English bone china, is to break it. He didn't have the heart to destroy our china. Or maybe he was a better psychologist than we took him for. When he discovered these dishes and what foods they had been used to serve, he suggested that we put them away. "Don't use them until I ask about such things in New York. Someone in New York must have more experience with things like this than I do."

They were put away. Every time he returned from a New York trip, Gail would ask what he had learned. And each time he had "forgotten." But he would be sure to remember next time. In the meantime, "Make sure they are put away in a safe place. You haven't used them, have you?"

This went on for months; then for years. The china was on display but it was never used. We kept waiting for expert advice that never came. Somehow, life went on without Minton Twilight in Grey.

We became closer to the Fellers during those years. Slowly the transformation which started in the kitchen moved into other areas of our life. Rabbi Feller introduced us to the Lubavitcher Rebbe, and we started growing in observance. Gail stopped singing in the synagogue choir; I started to put on *tefillin* sporadically at first, a little more regularly later on. I stopped driving on Shabbat. A few months later, so did Gail. We stopped eating at McDonalds. One Shabbat, we didn't switch on the television altogether. We bought a pair of *tzitzit* for the little boy. We switched membership to a synagogue with a *mechitzah* separating the men from the women. Gail started going to immerse in the *mikvah* (ritual bath). A few steps forward; a little backsliding; more steps forward. Years.

But the English bone china remained in the cabinet. Until one day, I came home from the university, and it was gone . . .

It was after a series of traumatic and melancholy miscarriages. Before observing *taharat ha'mishpacha* (the laws of family purity), it seems we had no difficulty having healthy and normal children. But when the *mikvah* became a feature of our family life, we started having trouble—three miscarriages in four years. Gail was sad; I was sad. Our friends comforted us. The Rebbe wrote letters of encouragement to Gail—private letters which I still have not read. But when I came home that singular day, she was smiling again:

"I took the china next door and sold it to Dorothy (our Gentile neighbor). Then I took the money and bought this *shaitel* (wig). What do you think of it?"

All this happened about 15 years ago. In 15 years you buy and discard a lot of *shaitlach*. Our two older daughters grew up and got married. They live with their husbands and their own children in Jerusalem. The little boy recently completed his rabbinic studies in the Lubavitch yeshiva in Montreal. We had two more children since

then—the delights of our middle age. We have grown, both of us, both personally and professionally.

And we have another set of English bone china, from which we eat every Shabbat.

B'Or Ha'Torah Journal: Science, Art and Modern Life in the Light of Torah, 6 (1987): 167-171
www.borhatorah.org, info@borhatorah.org
Reprinted with permission of the publisher

The Human Biosphere

by **Rabbi Yanki Tauber**

Land animals, which were created from the soil, are rendered fit to eat by the severing of both vital passages (the windpipe and the gullet). Fish, which were created from the water, do not require any shechitah *to render them fit to eat. Birds, which were created from a mixture of soil and water, are rendered fit to eat with the severing of either one of the two vital passages* (Talmud, Chulin 27b).

In the terminology of Kabbalah and Chassidism, "soil" and "water" are analogs for materiality and spirituality. Aside from the usual association of soil with earthiness and mundanity, and of water with purity and sublimity, soil and water express one of the basic distinguishing characteristics between matter and spirit. Soil is comprised of distinct granules, while water forms a cohesive expanse. When two types of soil (or any two solids[1] are combined, they remain separate entities, however thoroughly mixed; liquids, on the other hand, blend to the point of indistinguishability.[2] Indeed, the way to fuse solid particles to an integral whole is either to introduce

---

[1] The four basic elements, soil, water, air and fire, also represent the four states of matter—solid, liquid, gas and energy.

[2] This mechanical fact also has halachic implications—see Shulchan Aruch and commentaries, Yoreh Deah, 109.

a liquid element (as in the kneading of dough), or to heat them to the point of liquidity (as in welding).

By the same token, materiality tends to plurality and divisiveness, while the hallmark of the spiritual, is unity and oneness. The material world presents us with a great diversity of creatures, elements and forces, each bent on the preservation and enhancement of its individual existence. The material being is egocentric in essence, striving to consume whatever it needs (or merely desires) for itself, and resisting all attempts to consume it. While there are instances of cooperation and symbiosis in the material world, these are always toward the aim of mutual benefit rather than altruistic unity; furthermore, even this usually represents a triumph of mind over matter, and must be enforced upon a resisting egocentric instinct (witness the clash of egos in a marriage or the race and class-related tensions in a society).

On the other hand, spirituality, like water, is characterized by unity and cohesiveness, and, like water, is an agent of unity when introduced into the soil of the material. The soul amalgamates a diversity of cells and limbs into a "life"; the idea connects a myriad of disjointed facts into a cogent whole; love (that is, spiritual, altruistic love) supplants the instinctive "me" with a common "we." And when man shifts the focus of his life from the pursuit of material gratification to the service of his Creator, the diverse and belligerent granules of material life coalesce to a singular flow, as his every act and endeavor becomes an exercise in bringing harmony to the world and uniting it with its supernal source.

Beast, Fowl and Fish

The laws of kashrut, commanded by the Torah (primarily in Leviticus 11 and Deuteronomy 14) and interpreted and expounded upon in the Talmud (particularly in the tractate Chulin), establish which foods are permitted to the Jew, and which are forbidden. In regard to the consumption of animals, the laws of kashrut distinguish between three categories of animal: a) land animals, b) birds, and c) fish.[3]

One of the halachic distinctions among these three groups regards the requirement of *shechitah*, "slaughtering." Once an animal is determined to be kosher,[4] an array of laws govern how it may be slaughtered—the smallest nick in the knife, or the slightest deviation from the prescribed manner of slaughtering, renders the animal *tereif* and unfit for consumption. However, these laws differ from category to category. The most stringent *shechitah* requirements pertain to the "land animal": the slaughtering knife must cut through a majority of both of two vital passages, the windpipe and the gullet. At the other end of the spectrum are fish, which require no *shechitah* at all. Birds occupy the middle ground between land animals and fish: they do require *shechitah*, but the severing of (a majority of) only one of the vital passages—either the windpipe or the gullet—is sufficient.

The Talmud explains these differences as related to the primordial origins of these three categories of animals. Land animals were created from the earth (Genesis 1:24), and thus require a full-fledged *shechitah*; fish were created out of water (ibid., verse 20), and therefore do not require any *shechitah*; birds, which were created from a mixture of earth and water (ibid., and 2:19[5]), require the "lesser" *shechitah* prescribed for them.

What is the connection? Why is it that the "earthier" a creature is, the greater the need for *shechitah*? To understand this, we must first examine how all of the above applies to the inner world of the human soul. "Man is a universe in miniature,"[6] our sages have said, echoing King Solomon's adage, "Also the world He placed in their hearts"[7]; if there are three categories of animal life on the macrocosmic level, the same is true of man—our interior biosphere also includes the land beast, the water creature, and the earth/water composite that rides the winds. Here, too, the laws of kashrut and *shechitah* apply, instructing us how to distinguish the desirable from the undesirable in our psyche, and how to make

---

[3] These three groups each have a different set of criteria for distinction between kosher and non-kosher animals. For a land animal to be kosher, it must chew its cud and have split hooves; in practice, this means that only ten species of land animal are permitted for consumption. With birds, the situation is

reversed: the Torah lists twenty species of non-kosher birds and permits all others. Finally, kosher fish are distinguished by two "signs"—fins and scales.

[4] See previous note.

[5] See Talmud, Chulin 27b.

[6] Midrash Tanchuma, Pikudei 3.

[7] Ecclesiastes 3:11.

its "kosher" elements fit for consumption and metabolization in the daily process of life.

The Three Souls of Man

In the opening chapters of Tanya, the "bible" of Chabad Chassidism, Rabbi Schneur Zalman of Liadi establishes that we each possess two distinct souls: the "animal soul" (*nefesh habehamit*)[8] and the "G-dly soul" (*nefesh ha'elokit*).[9] The animal soul is the essence of physical life. Its focus is entirely self-oriented, its every act and desire motivated by the quest for self-fulfillment and self-enhancement; in this, the animal soul shares the nature of every physical being, whose most basic tendency is the preservation and betterment of its own existence. In contradistinction, the essence of the "G-dly soul" is the striving to unite with its source, to be nullified within the all-pervading reality of G-d. Were this striving to be fully realized, the G-dly soul would cease to exist as a distinct entity[10]; nevertheless, such is its nature and desire. This makes for the perpetual struggle of life: the struggle between matter and spirit, between self-assertion and self-transcendence. Any thought, desire, or act of man stems from either of his two souls, depending upon which has gained mastery over the other and is asserting itself in the person's mind, heart and behavior.

Chassidic teaching also speaks of a third, intermediary soul in every man—a soul less subjective than his animal soul, though not quite as transcendent as his G-dly soul. This is the *nefesh hasichlit*, the "intellectual soul." The intellect of man is the most transcendent element of his natural self, capable of objective thought and self-examination. This is not to say that the intellect is entirely free of the inhibitions of ego and self-interest; but it at least possesses the capacity to conceive of greater realities, and thus perceive the insignificance of the self before a higher truth. The intellectual self is thus the bridge between the G-dly soul, which strives toward a self-obliterating union with G-d, and the animal self, which is blind to everything save the gratification of its egocentric instincts. It is via the intellectual soul that the G-dly soul can influence the animal soul: when a person gains a recognition of the divine truth and an appreciation of the purpose to which he was created, this very knowledge and understanding serves to refine his character and behavior.[11]

These are the beast, bird, and water-creature within man. The animal soul of man is the "land animal" in man[12]—a wholly material being, individualistic and self-engrossed as the soil from which it is fashioned. At the other end of the spectrum is the wholly spiritual G-dly soul, characterized by the unity and adhesiveness of the water from which it derives. The G-dly soul of man also resembles the water creature in that it lives wholly immersed in its source—just as a fish cannot survive outside of the water that spawned it, so, too, the G-dly soul cannot conceive of an existence apart from its divine source.[13] In the words of Rabbi Schneur Zalman of Liadi, the G-dly essence of man, "never desires, nor is it ever capable of distancing itself from G-d," so that "even at the very moment a person sins, his quintessential self remains loyal to G-d,"[14] taking no part in the deed—it has merely been suppressed and overwhelmed by his animal self.

Then there is the "bird" in man: a creature fashioned from soil and water, an admixture of matter and spirit. A creature that is capable of soaring to the most sublime heights, though it repeatedly returns to earth to rest and feed between flights. This is the intellect of man, capable, on the one hand, of raising itself above the materiality of earth and attaining a higher vantage point on life and

---

[8] The word *beheimah* actually means "beast" or "land animal" (see Rashi on Deuteronomy 14:5); thus, a more precise translation of *nefesh habehamit* would be the "beastly soul" or the "land-animal soul."

[9] The concept of a "good inclination" (*yetzer tov*) and "evil inclination" (*yetzer hara*) in the heart of man abounds in the Talmud and the Midrashim (cf. Talmud, Berachot 61a). What is unique about the Tanya's thesis (which is based on the teachings of Rabbi Chaim Vital, a disciple of master Kabbalist Rabbi Isaac Luria) is that it speaks of two *souls*—two entire personas, each with a full set of traits and faculties. The two "inclinations" are actually the drives and desires of their respective souls.

[10] This is the deeper significance of what happened to Nadav and Avihu, who "came close to G-d, and died" (Leviticus 16:1; see ibid., 10:1-7). In the words of Rabbi Chaim ibn Atar, theirs was "a death by divine 'kiss' like that experienced by the perfectly righteous—it is only that the righteous die when the divine kiss approaches them, while they died by their approaching it.... Although they sensed their own demise, this did not prevent them from drawing near [to G-d] in attachment, delight, delectability, fellowship, love, kiss and sweetness, to the point that their souls ceased from them." (Ohr Hachaim commentary on verse).

---

[11] Likkutei Torah, Bechukotai 47c-48a; Sefer Hamaamarim 5702, pp. 106-109.

[12] See note 8 above.

[13] See Talmud, Berachot 61b.

[14] Tanya, ch. 24. See Mishneh Torah, Laws of Divorce, 2:20.

self, yet nevertheless bound, in many ways, to the physical reality of which it is part.

Drawing Forth

Before an animal can be eaten, to become the stuff of our bodies and the motor of our lives, two conditions must be met: it must be determined to be kosher, and it must undergo *shechitah* as dictated by Torah law.

"*Shechitah* is only to draw forth,"[15] states the Talmud. The most basic meaning of this rule is that the slaughtering knife must be *drawn across* the "vital passages"—pressing downward, or other deviations from the required back-and-forth movement, disqualify the *shechitah*. Chassidic teaching, however, uncovers the deeper significance of this law: that the function of *shechitah* is to "draw forth"—to draw the animal out from its beastly state and into the domain of a life consecrated to the service of the Creator. This is achieved by "slaughtering" the beast—i.e., taking its life. The material world is not, in itself, a negative thing; what is negative is material *life*—the passion and zeal for things material. The Jew knows that while "the entire world was created to serve me," "I was created to serve my Creator"[16]—the reason why man has been granted mastery over the physical world is that he utilize it in his fulfillment of the divine will. Man was created to live a spiritual life that is sustained by the material, not a material life which his spiritual prowess has been harnessed to serve; to crave the physical for its own sake, is to become part of it rather than to make it part of you and a partner to your transcendent goals. So even after man has separated the "kosher" aspects of life from non-kosher ones, rejecting all that is irredeemable and corrupting,[17] he must still "slaughter" the material beast before it can be consumed. Only after its "life" has been taken out of it can it be sublimated as an accessory to the life of the spirit.

Hence the differing *shechitah* requirements for the three components of inner life of man. The "animal soul" requires a full-fledged *shechitah*: comprised solely of the soil of materialism, it must be drained of all vitality and passion so that its substance might be "drawn forth" into the realm of holiness. The "intellectual soul," comprised of both "soil" and "water," requires a partial *shechitah*—its material and egotistic elements must be subdued, but there remains much about the intellect that is desirable also in its "animated" form. [18]Finally, the wholly selfless, wholly transcendent "G-dly soul" requires no *shechitah* at all, for both its substance and spirit are desirable and "digestible" elements in the life of man.

Based on the Rebbe's writings, including a letter dated, Tishrei 25, 5703 (October 6, 1942) and a journal entry marked "Shechitah. Vichy. 5700" (1940-41)[19]
www.meaningfullife.com
Reprinted with permission

Is Kosher Food Safer?

by **Deborah Kotz**

Not only Jews look for the kosher symbol on food these days. In a surprising turn of events, "kosher" has become the most popular claim on new food products, trouncing "organic" and "no additives or preservatives," according to a recent report. A noteworthy 4,719 new kosher items were launched in the United States last year—nearly double the number of new "all natural" products, which placed second in the report, issued last month by Mintel, a Chicago-based market research firm.

In fact, sales of kosher foods have risen an estimated 15 percent a year for the past decade. Yet Jews, whose

---

[15] *Ein v'shachat ela umashach*—Talmud, Chulin 30b. Thus, *shechitah* is equated with the halachic concept of *meshicah*, which effects the transfer of an object from on domain to another.

[16] Talmud, Kiddushin 82a.

[17] Indeed, there are non-kosher elements in all three categories, including the utterly selfless "fish." For while the G-dly soul's self-abnegation before G-d is its highest virtue, there also exists a negative type of self-abnegation, as in the case of one who lacks the pride and self-assurance necessary to resist those persons and forces that seek to prevent his doing what is right. In chassidic terminology such a tendency is called *askufah hanidresses*, or a "doormat personality."

[18] This is also why there are more non-kosher land animals than kosher ones, while the reverse is true of birds (see note 3 above).

[19] Igrot Kodesh, vol. I, pp. 46-48; Reshimot #23, pp. 5-10

---

religious doctrine mandates the observance of kosher dietary laws, make up only 20 percent of those buying kosher products. What gives? "It's the belief among all consumers that kosher food is safer, a critical thing right now with worries about the integrity of the food supply," says Marcia Mogelonsky, a senior research analyst at Mintel.

Whether kosher foods are actually less likely to be contaminated with, say, *E. coli* bacteria remains up for debate. While research is scant in this area, experts say it makes sense that kosher food could be safer because it's more closely monitored. "Jews aren't allowed to ingest bugs, so produce must go through a thorough washing and checking to ensure that no bugs are found within the leaves or on the surface of the fruit or vegetable," says Moshe Elefant, a rabbi and chief operating officer of the Orthodox Union, a kosher certification organization based in New York. But bacteria can remain even after this type of washing, so consumers can't assume they're less likely to get food poisoning with bagged spinach marked kosher than with a conventional bag.

The same caveat applies to poultry and beef. A salting process that removes blood from the meat has antibacterial effects, but salmonella and *E. coli* can still survive, says Joe Regenstein, a professor of food science who teaches a course on Jewish and Muslim food laws at Cornell University. Kosher beef, though, is much less likely to contain the misshapen proteins that cause mad cow disease, rare as that is, probably because the animals are slaughtered young, before the disease sets in.

Another selling point of kosher foods is that they're easily decoded by those looking to avoid dairy or meat. "One of the fundamental rules of kosher certification is that you can't mix meat and milk," says Elefant. So each product is labeled either dairy or meat—or "pareve" (also spelled parve) if it contains neither. Pareve foods can't even be manufactured on equipment previously used for dairy or meat products. "People with severe dairy allergies are looking for that pareve designation," Elefant says. They might also turn to kosher salami and hot dogs, since nonkosher cured meats often contain a preservative made from milk sugar, though [they] may simply buy kosher because they prefer the stricter supervision that goes into certifying kosher foods. "Food companies

agree to allow a third-party inspector to come in unannounced, at essentially any time," says Regenstein. These inspectors check, among other things, that products are being manufactured only with those ingredients listed on the label. Companies, he says, must carefully keep records of where ingredients come from—not always the case for small nonkosher food manufacturers—which allows for quick recall if a product gets contaminated with a nonkosher ingredient or food-borne pathogen. "That alone is worth the price of kosher," Regenstein opines. Contrary to what some folks think, however, a rabbi doesn't bless the food. "Kosher dietary laws are actually just a simple set of rules," explains Elefant, "and the kosher certification helps those who make a commitment to live under those rules."

U.S. News and World Report, January 11, 2008
Reprinted with permission of the publisher

Spiritual Molecules

by **Dr. Velvl Greene**

Most of us "believe" in molecules.

Hardly any one of us has ever seen a molecule, and unless we have studied a lot of chemistry and physics and physical chemistry, we probably don't understand the tests and criteria used by scientists to detect molecules, analyze them, identify them or describe their structure. Still, we believe they exist, have definable structures, weights and shapes and possess predictable properties. We have been taught that all molecules are made up of a hundred or so elemental atoms—just as all words are made up of the same basic letters. The countless and varied molecules that make up our physical world differ from each other only with respect to the type of atoms they contain, the numbers of atoms present, their pattern of organization and their location in the molecular structure—just as all of the words in our language differ from each other only with respect to the letters they contain and their sequence. And the same words can be used to write a psalm or a political pamphlet—just as the same molecules can be found in an ant or an elephant.

There is nothing mystical about this anymore. It isn't imaginary or hypothetical. The concept of molecules and atoms and their reactions is as accepted as are things we can see and judge with our own senses.

If a chemist tells us that a given molecule has three carbon atoms and another molecule has six, we believe him. If the chemist tells us that the six carbon atoms of one molecule are in a ring, while in another molecule they are forked, we believe him. Sometimes we believe because it makes sense. More often, we believe because we have no reason to disbelieve. Most of the time we believe because we have a basic confidence in the chemist's honesty and competence.

Chemists and their colleagues have more credibility in our eyes than merchants, lawyers and most of the public servants we choose to run our country. And much of the confidence is justified. Molecular theory and manipulation are the very basis of the exciting discoveries being made almost daily in physiology, genetics, microbiology and pharmacology. The chemist has used his molecular models quite effectively to make predictions and products that have changed our lives.

For example, people long ago discovered, by empirical trial and error, that certain foods were nutritious while others were poisonous; certain beverages were intoxicating while others were innocuous; certain diets were fattening while others, which also satisfied hunger, were less so. In the early years of this century nutritionists learned that the absence of certain foodstuffs from normal diets resulted in pathological consequences. About the same time, allergists learned that adding certain ingredients to normal diets also resulted in pathological consequences. It wasn't until the chemists provided us with "metabolic maps" that we started to sort out the mass of confusing empirical data. These metabolic maps described the molecular pathways involved in food digestion and cell synthesis. They showed how the complex minerals, proteins carbohydrates and lipids present in our dietary foodstuffs could be broken down

into simpler and simpler molecules; concurrently, these simple molecules could be utilized by our own bodies for putting together the proteins, minerals, carbohydrates and lipids that constitute our tissues. The maps showed how the whole process was regulated by other molecules (vitamins). The molecular models explained how and why certain foods generated toxic responses and other foods generated allergic responses; the bases of some classical deficiency diseases like rickets, pellagra, goiter and beriberi; the rationale of weight-reducing diets; and dozens of other physiological and pharmacological phenomena.

It can be fairly said that molecular chemistry and molecular biology established nutrition, physiology and nutritional pathology as sciences and took them out of the grasp of alchemists and quacks.

Kashrut and Chemistry

Thoughts of this nature kept intruding as I was reviewing the Torah portion *Shemini* (Leviticus 9-10), wherein the Jewish people were commanded, eternally, to avoid certain foods while being permitted to consume others.

The Torah itself gives no reason for these laws. But anyone familiar with the modern molecular theories of nutrition and nutritional pathology can hardly avoid the temptation of creating molecular models and maps to explain everything in this field.

But it is futile speculation . . .

In his classic volume on biblical and talmudic medicine, written 73 years ago. Dr. Julius Preuss introduced his discussion on kashrut (dietary laws) with the following statement:

> The biblical dietary laws are included in the chapter on "Hygiene" solely because we can conceive of no reason other than sanitary for their ordination. It must be emphasized, however, that the Torah gives us no reason at all for these laws and the later sources do so only rarely. Thus, nearly everything which one alleges to be the reason for the dietary

laws is only a hypothesis and is read into the sources . . .

This statement establishes precisely the frustrating paradox confronting anyone who would like to explain the laws of kashrut using modern knowledge of nutrition and public health as a model. We don't know why certain animals, birds and fish are permitted for food while others are banned; we don't know why the permitted quadrupeds and birds must be slaughtered in a given fashion; we don't know why blood, certain fatty tissues and the sciatic nerve are forbidden; we don't know the hazards associated with cooking and/or consuming meat and milk; and we don't know why certain specific anatomical imperfections render an animal or fowl *traifa* (not kosher) and thus prohibited. We are provided with remarkably detailed guides and instructions about the criteria that distinguish between prohibited and acceptable, but nothing about why. Though we very much want to know why, any rational explanation is simply an exercise in human imagination.

The greatest minds ever produced by the human race have struggled for thousands of years to explain these laws. Dozens, if not hundreds of hypotheses have been proposed to elucidate these mysteries. Why is the ox kosher and the camel not? Why cannot a Jew eat pork and benefit from the well-known nutritional quality of swine flesh? Why is carp acceptable while eels are not? The rational mind yearns to understand and unfortunately, because it cannot understand, sometimes decides to ignore the laws altogether!

In the last hundred years or so, it has become fashionable to explain kashrut with analogies from public health. The basic argument is that Moses was really a primitive health commissioner, and the Parshah of *Shemini* was an early model of current Pure Food and Drug laws. It is an intriguing concept, but its adherents today are mainly Jews who do not want to observe the dietary restrictions in the first place. Very little support for this point of view will be found in authentic public health research. Rabbits are as nutritious as chickens; gefilte fish can be made as well from sturgeon as from trout; there isn't that much difference—microbiologically or chemically—between lamb and pork.

It would be easier to understand (and adhere to?) the dietary restrictions if we would find a chemical reason. It would be easier particularly if we could isolate some kind of substance or harmful chemical from a forbidden food that is not present in a permitted food. Or if we could show that the processes described in the *Shulchan Aruch* (Code of Jewish Law) inhibit some obscure molecular reaction which produces a toxin. That would make sense. We have a lot of empirical experience with food poisoning and allergies. Undoubtedly our ancestors did also. There are certain foodstuffs in nature that are intrinsically poisonous—certain mushrooms, for example, some fish and some mollusks. It would be quite reasonable for a primitive lawmaker to ban them as food for his tribe. We also know that foods, if improperly stored or processed, can become vehicles for transmission of infectious agents or their toxins. Thus a primitive lawgiver, concerned with the physical health of his tribe, would also ordain laws about processing and storing the materials which have been permitted as food.

If non-kosher foods or improper processing resulted in food poisoning or infection or skin eruptions, we could understand.

But they really don't. From a nutritional and toxicological perspective, there is no difference between a kosher and non-kosher diet. The answer certainly is not chemical. It isn't the physical atoms and molecules of pork that render it inedible for Jews. Otherwise, why is it not forbidden to non-Jews? Is it possible that there are chemical receptors or Jewish cells that are sensitive to molecules of *traifa* foods? It is not beyond medical experience. Some humans are allergic to strawberries while others are not. Indeed, the only difference between the allergic and the retractile is a subtle molecular reaction that occurs in the former and not in the latter. A better example might be the genetic (some say racial) inability of some humans to digest bovine milk while others literally thrive on it. Thus there are molecular reactions, in the realm of nutritional pathology and which are hereditary that can serve as a justification for dietary taboos.

Unfortunately, it doesn't wash clean. Jewish racial qualities are more a Nazi myth than a chemical reality today. When the dietary prohibitions were announced, the 12 tribes encamped around Sinai several thousand years ago certainly shared a similar genetic make up. But in the thousands of years since then and particularly in the thousands of years of diaspora, the genetic homogeneity became significantly diluted. Jews today differ greatly in blood types and immunological make up and physiological response to nutrients. Today a chemical explanation of kashrut—which remains extremely binding despite the gradual genetic diversification is—simply an inadequate hypothesis. A convert to Judaism is obligated to observe the kashrut laws as soon as she or he becomes a Jew, even if he or she has thrived physiologically on the now-forbidden foods until that very moment.

Spiritual Molecules

Many of the rabbinic commentators make reference, while humbly denying that they know the true answer, to the "spiritual damage" that derives from non-kosher foods. For example. Rabbi Shimshon Raphael Hirsch comments on the Torah portion *Kedoshim* (Leviticus 19-20) as follows:

> You must . . . conscientiously keep . . . the choice of nourishment . . . as the very first preliminary . . . for spiritual, mental and moral clarity, purity and holiness . . . right from the beginning, at the actual forming of the tissues of your body, the physical formation of the fibers of your brain, nerves and muscles . . .

The forbidden foods are thus not materially poisonous, but they are harmful to our soul. The dangerous components of pork cannot be detected by chemists, and the toxicological effects of its consumption cannot be diagnosed by physicians, but the damage does certainly occur. If we want to think in terms of molecules, we must think about "spiritual molecules."

In this respect, I once read that there are spiritual poisons in certain proscribed foods that dull the spiritual senses or, as is put so well in Yiddish, "stuff up the nose and ears of the soul" to the extent that the individual can no longer receive spiritual messages. I also heard that the animals forbidden as food by Torah possess certain spiritual characteristics which the consumer is in danger of acquiring. Whatever the rationale, spiritual molecules make more sense than chemical ones.

But they make sense only to one who already believes in the authority of Torah and that person is already willing to obey the rules without any rationalizations. To the rest of the world, spiritual molecules are too much the subject of mystery and superstition. In the spiritual realm, according to those who consider themselves modern and scientific there are no rules and no logic—just a lot of fairy stories, visions, magic, witchcraft and gurus.

Of course, real molecules are also invisible and intangible to most of us. Real molecules are also the subjects of speculation by the gurus (of science) who wear their priestly garments and who officiate in their esoteric temples (called laboratories) after years of apprenticeship. But spiritual molecules are too much for the twentieth century.

(Parenthetically, I wonder if our rabbis would be more successful in getting their message across if they exchanged their black frocks for white lab coats? I wonder if the observance of kashrut would be enhanced by impressive lab equipment and periodic tables and diagrams of covalent electron bonds or their spiritual equivalent? Probably not. The contemporary Jewish non-observer is too sophisticated for that; he wouldn't fall for such gimmicks. If he doesn't obey the rules when G-d Himself issues them, why would he change because a rabbi put on a white coat?

Then why does he believe in molecules made up of carbon atoms? But that's another story . . .)

I submit that the real barrier to accepting the role of spiritual molecules derives from two handicaps in conceptualization:

1) The lack of immediate empirical proof of spiritual harm when the laws are disregarded;

2) The matter of particularism, i.e., the selective nature of the dietary laws which permit the majority of humans to eat and benefit from a given food while denying the same opportunity to a very small group of people who are indistinguishable in any detectable way from the majority and who also seem to benefit from the food.

PKU—a Medical Model of Kashrut?

We are taught in Chassidism that the spiritual world and the material world are parallels of each other. Thus phenomena experienced in the flesh and blood universe are modeled on spiritual phenomena. Similarly, the spiritual universe is reflected in things and events which are detected by our mortal senses.

This permits us to postulate the existence of spiritual molecules based on our knowledge of chemical structures. Indeed, there are those who would say that the material molecules we study and teach about in chemistry courses are really the reflection of the intangible spiritual molecules the Creator used as a blueprint!

With this in mind I present the natural history of a rare genetic disease that might provide some kind of answer to those who reject kashrut because they lack empirical proof of harm and feel uncomfortable with strict particularism.

Medicine is familiar with a condition called phenylketonuria or PKU. First described fifty years ago, this hereditary metabolic disorder affects about one out of 15,000 children born in the northern hemisphere and leads, among other things, to an irreversible and severe retardation.

The newborn child appears healthy and normal. He cannot really be distinguished during a routine physical examination, from his 14,999 unaffected peers. He has a normal appetite and an apparently unremarkable metabolism. He eats, sleeps, cries and does all of the other things babies are expected to do. But gradually—over the course of several years—he develops a characteristic appearance and brain damage.

Many years after the disease was first described, physiologists determined that the brain damage was a result of the accumulation in the body of a certain amino acid—phenylalanine—which is a common molecule in many proteins. Normal people have the ability to metabolize phenylalanine and to convert it to other, non-harmful (and essential) nutrients. But one child in 15,000 lacks the necessary enzyme and the phenylalanine

accumulates and accumulates until it harms the developing brain.

About 35 years ago, a chemist named Guthrie described a blood test which permits the early diagnosis of PKU, within a few days after birth, long before the neurological damage has occurred. This test is now compulsory in most Western countries (including Israel). Every baby born in a hospital is tested for PKU. If the results suggest that the condition is present, the mother is provided with nutritional advice and counseling. If the diet is modified early enough, if the phenylalanine-containing protein is replaced with a synthetic substitute and fed for the first four or five years, the retardation can usually be avoided. The solution isn't simple; it is also inconvenient, unappetizing and expensive. But, it is effective.

Now consider the following scenario: a public health nurse visits a young mother who has just come home from the hospital with her precious newborn baby. The nurse conveys the frightening news that according to the lab tests the baby has PKU. She also provides the mother with a list of prescribed foods and instructions for preparing a suitable preventive diet.

Neither the nurse nor the mother is a chemist. The mother knows nothing about molecules or physiology or metabolism. She knows what she sees—a healthy, normal baby, like any other baby in the world, who enjoys eating and is apparently thriving on the diet being provided. The nurse knows a little more. She has studied a little chemistry and understands the best physiology of metabolism. Or at least, she believes the teachers who taught her. The nurse doesn't really know the basis of the diagnostic tests; nor could she prescribe a diet out of her own experience. All she is doing is her job of transmitting the information she was taught. She believes she is acting in the best interests of the child and the community. But she is mostly acting out of duty and acceptance of higher authorities—such as doctors, chemist and nutritionists—who have studied more and know more and have better sources of knowledge.

The mother refuses to accept the diagnosis or the diet. She doesn't believe in the mysteries of chemistry or accept the authority of the doctors. Doesn't her baby look normal? Isn't the baby happy? Besides, the recommended diet is too expensive and inconvenient and unappetizing. What is all this nonsense about molecules anyway?

I end with the following question:

If you were the nurse, what would you do when the mother demands, "Show me the danger now! Show me the difference between my baby and all the others!"

B'Or Ha'Torah Journal: Science, Art and Modern Life in the Light of Torah 6 (1987): 159-164
www.borhatorah.org, info@borhatorah.org
Reprinted with permission of the publisher

Holy Shibuta
A Fishy Tale for Rosh Hashana

by **Rabbi Dr. Ari Z. Zivotofsky** and **Dr. Ari Greenspan**

Imagine the great talmudic scholar Rava, his mouth watering, thinking about the next bite of his Shabbat meal and knowing that it will taste like ham. That image is what brought us to a most unusual meal, sitting in a forest overlooking the Euphrates River in Turkey. We dined with the provincial governor and a fish expert from the University of Harran with the apt name of Zafer Dogu, while we munched on a fish that in Arabic is called *shabut*.

Our main quest on this journey that had brought us to south central Turkey was for lesser-known Jewish customs and traditions, and while trawling for Jewish lore just 60 km. north of the Syrian border, we hit the mother lode. To understand this fish's tale, a bit of seining of the traditional sources is needed.

As we sit down to our Rosh Hashana meal, Jews all around the world begin their first course with foods that symbolize hopefulness and dreams of happiness and peace for the coming year. The most common custom is the dipping of an apple into honey, symbolizing that the impending year should be sweet. A less well known custom, but one with venerable and ancient roots, is dipping a ram's head in honey as a reminder of the binding of Isaac and the anticipation of a pleasant year.

Another common custom is to eat the head of a fish or ram, upon which we pronounce our desire that "we should be as a head and not as a tail." Many people also eat fish and recite "may it be Your will, our God Who is the God of our fathers, that we increase and multiply like fish."

The fish in Judaism is seen as a particularly common and positive symbol. Fish bear many offspring and are a symbol of fertility. The protective shield used by *mohelim*, ritual circumcisers, is often made in the shape of a fish because it represents fertility. The body of water where we say *tashlich*, the symbolic "casting of our sins into the sea," during this High Holy Day season, ideally should contain fish because fish are considered immune to the "evil eye." Because of this, fish is also the symbol of the month of Adar.

As opposed to animals, birds and grasshoppers, no fish are named in the entire Bible. Talmudic literature does mention several species by their common names, with the fish mentioned most often being the *shibuta*. Whatever this shibuta was, it was well known by the Diaspora community of Babylonia of old.

The Talmud discusses shibuta in several contexts. We are told that the great sages of the Talmud rolled up their sleeves and involved themselves directly in preparations for the Shabbat. The amora Rava would personally salt the shibuta fish for the Shabbat meal. We surmise from this that the fish was well known and considered enough of a delicacy to be served for the Sabbath repast.

It is described as both having medicinal value or posing a health risk, depending on the season of the year and the medical condition involved. A salted head of shibuta boiled in beer is a cure for a disease called *yarkona* (jaundice?). On the other hand, according to the Gemara, eating the shibuta during the spring month of Nisan could cause leprosy.

One of the more interesting references has to do with the unique taste of the creature. The Talmud relates that for everything that God prohibited in this world, He also created a counterpart that was permitted. For example, blood is prohibited, but the liver, which contains an abundance of the vital fluid, was permitted. Even though milk and meat may not be eaten together, the udder of a lactating cow is permissible.

Now here's the kicker. The pig, the most detestable of animals to the Jewish people, is of course forbidden as food. However, should one have a penchant to taste the forbidden swine, we are informed that the flavor of pork is identical to (part of) the shibuta.

For the last few centuries the identity of the talmudic shibuta has puzzled European scholars and at least a half dozen possible species have been proposed. But it is no longer a mystery for us. Having an interest in Jewish culinary traditions, several years ago I asked an Iraqi-born Tel Aviv cab driver which kosher birds they used to eat in his native land. When the nostalgia of his youth warmed his soul, he smiled and said that by far the tastiest item in their cuisine was neither fowl nor meat, but a fish called the shabut. His response electrified me. Could his shabut in Arabic be the shibuta of the Talmud?

As I later discovered, the great rabbinic leader of Baghdadi Jewry from the early 20th century, Rabbi Yosef Haim (known as the Ben Ish Hai) had no doubt. He listed the five most common kosher fish eaten in Baghdad and after mentioning the shabut he says "that is the shibuta of the Talmud." So here was the shibuta—it is a type of carp known in Arabic as shabut and by the scientific name *Barbus grypus*, from the family *Cyprinidae* (carps and minnows). The Europeans were stymied because they were looking in Europe, while the shibuta of the Babylonian Talmud is obviously found in Babylonia, modern-day Iraq.

That taxi ride ignited a passion to behold and maybe even taste this talmudic delicacy. We turned to the largest collection of preserved fish in the country, a true national treasure located at Hebrew University in Jerusalem, but alas, it was lacking *shibuta*.

The next step would be more difficult and was our conundrum: The fish lives in the Tigris and Euphrates rivers, which flow through Iraq, Iran and Syria and are not readily accessible to Israelis. But with the help of several parties outside of Israel, we managed to get our first few shibuta shipped from its natural territory via a third country. The trouble was that they were preserved in formaldehyde, so we could not get a taste. A side benefit was that we were able to donate a *Barbus grypus* to the Hebrew University collection.

Our desire for a frozen sample to eat on Rosh Hashana was not quelled. Travel to Iraq, Iran and Syria may be difficult for us, but there are many US military and civilian personnel in Iraq and US army chaplain Lt.-Col. Jeremy Steinberg is among them. He had already served a tour of duty in Afghanistan and was serving his second tour in Iraq. Having known him for many years and knowing that he is good at detective work (he has a forthcoming book on Hebrew etymology), I e-mailed him about my search and finally convinced him that I was really serious about wanting him to find a shabut.

He agreed to look, though doubted that he would be successful. But succeed he did. He approached an Iraqi who was employed on the US Army base and asked him to find out about the possibility of getting a shabut for him. The base, being near the Euphrates and the shabut being popular, the Iraqi returned the next morning not with information but with a box containing two big and two small specimens. Chaplain Steinberg promptly purchased the fish, recorded the event with many pictures that quickly clogged my inbox, but alas the fish are still in Iraq because we have not found a legal means to ship them from there to Israel.

Our search was not over and took a positive turn when we "discovered" that the Tigris and Euphrates have their sources in a friendly country, Turkey. Quite fortuitously, I found not just a fish expert but a *Barbus grypus* expert, Dr. Zafer Dogu, from the Department of Fisheries, Bozova Vocational School, Harran University. He was more than glad to cooperate and find a few fish for us. But things improved even more when we contacted the Turkish embassy, which graciously assisted us with arrangements for our trip to study the shibuta in the Euphrates, just a stone's throw from Harran, the city of our forefather Abraham.

We flew to Istanbul and from there to Sanliurfa, landing on the longest runway in Turkey in a deserted, brand new airport that was opened only the previous week. One's initial impression upon arriving in this area near the Euphrates is that of the lush green patches irrigated by the majestic river among the otherwise moon-like landscape of the harsh arid region of south-central Turkey. We stepped out of the airport into 44-degree heat and proceeded to the office of Governor Mehmet Özel, who warmly welcomed us and assisted us with all of our needs.

After an initial meeting with the governor, the fish expert and his boss, we were taken to a lake that was formed when the Atatürk Dam on the Euphrates was completed in 1993. The dam, one of the largest in the world, is part of the massive $32 billion public project known as the Great Southeastern Anatolia Project (GAP) that has greatly improved the standard of living in the region. The lake covers 815 sq. km., and when it was filled for the first time it submerged 25 villages, displacing 55,000 inhabitants, and several important unexplored archeological sites.

Waiting for us on the lake were two boats that took us to the middle of this placid body of water, where we observed local fishermen pulling in nets full of fish. Unfortunately, none of the fish caught while we were there were shibuta. So as not to disappoint us, Dogu, took out and prepared (very cooperatively according to our instructions so that it remained kosher) one of the shibuta he had caught for us in advance, and a lovely lakeside "state dinner" with the governor was held. From there, we were taken to see the fish research facility where work is being done on raising, among other fish, the shibuta by, among others, Dogu who is a leading researcher on *Barbus grypus* sperm.

Perhaps the most interesting aspect of the story came to light when we reached our hotel, an old stone structure built right near an early Arab holy site called the Mosque of Abraham in the ancient part of Sanliurfa. According to Muslim tradition, King Nimrod was angered by Abraham having smashed his father's idols,

and had him catapulted into a fiery furnace. God in His benevolence miraculously caused the fire to turn into water and the logs into fish. And not just any fish, but shabut. On the site of the furnace-turned-pond an ancient church existed and then a mosque was built.

In 1896 this pool was visited by a Christian traveler who described the experience (See http://armenianhouse. org/harris/armenia/letter11.html):

> I was visiting, under guard of a Turkish soldier, the most beautiful part of Edessa, the fish-pond on the borders of which stands the Mosque of Abraham the friend of God, and a Moslem college. This college is the successor of the famous Christian school of Edessa, and the mosque, no doubt, marks the site of an ancient Christian church. The pool is full of fish, which it is prohibited under severe penalty to kill, and which every one feeds with bread and pennyworths of parched corn. Such a rush when you throw it in! They tumble over one another, and jump half out of the water. Obviously the protection and support which the fish enjoy comes from a time when they were considered sacred. So I asked my soldier what was the name of the fish, and his answer was, "In Arabic they are called shabut."

This was not the end of the story. It was time to take a fish to Los Angeles for an OU "halachic dinner" to share with the rest of the Jewish world (see http://www. greenspandental.com/JewishJournal.com.html). But how could we get the fish into the US legally and with it staying fresh? This turned out to not be a concern. We were informed in an e-mail by the deputy chief of Trade Operations, Customs and Border Protection of the Port Authority of New York and New Jersey that "non living fish [from Turkey] that are for personal consumption and free from live pests/insects are not regulated and permitted entry."

Dogu's boss, Asst. Prof. Erdinç Sahinöz confirmed the health status of our fish. Going through security is often a tense experience. In the isolated, new empty Sanliurfa airport, the security people sat up straight in their chairs and their eyes popped when they saw a large fish on the

X-ray scanner. A lot of explaining and laughing went on in security offices that day, and we gave a new meaning to flying fish. They found it so amusing (and we were the only passengers in sight) that they even permitted us to photograph the X-ray of the shibuta.

Had our Turkish been better, we might have found dry ice in Istanbul, but given its current state our precious cargo was wrapped in regular ice, hand carried and stored in the overhead bins, and off we went. The dripping water we explained to fellow passengers must be faulty air-conditioning units on the planes, and we headed to LA hoping for the best. It arrived still frozen, was masterfully prepared by the chef at the Prime Grill with applesauce, instead of an apple in its mouth, and was willingly consumed at the Baron Herzog winery in Oxnard by a group of OU rabbis.

The question we are often asked is "does it taste like pig?" Having never tasted pork, we cannot personally answer that question. But the final verdict of the chef at the Prime Grill, after finding commonality between their textures and consistency, was a definite "no."

What is interesting is that three different texts exist regarding the exact description of the shibuta's taste. One source says the fish tastes like pig. Another says its brain does, and a third states the tongue is the tasty morsel. Could the rabbis have been talking tongue in cheek? As any angler will tell you, the tongue or brain of a small freshwater fish is so tiny as to be almost nonexistent.

Might the lesson be more along the lines of being satisfied with what we have and transmitting to us that we should not feel as if we are missing anything in this world? Basically, the lesson might be that if you feel like you are lacking, search far and hard enough and you might even find what you thought you never could.

As of now, the shibuta does not live in Israel. However, it has the potential to, and indeed some of its close relatives do. Two such species are *Barbus longiceps*, a species that exists nowhere else except the Kinneret and its tributaries, and *Barbus canis*, a fish found in the Jordan River. This brings us to a beautiful midrash.

As we start a new year and dream of peace and prosperity and of the days to come, let us contemplate the eschatological message that the rabbis tell us the shibuta has the potential to share with us. The midrash allegorically tells us that when the Jews went into exile at the hands of the Babylonians, "700 types of kosher fish, 800 types of kosher locusts and an unlimited number of kosher birds were exiled with them to Babylonia, and when they returned all of them returned with them except for the fish called the shibuta . . . and in the days to come, all are destined to return."

Shana Tova to all, and a year of great fishing, wherever your pond may be.

The Jerusalem Post, September 17, 2007
Reprinted with permission of the publisher

Lesson 3

Beyond the Nose Job
Judaism, the Body, and the Bedroom

Introduction

In this lesson, we will discuss when 2 = 1 and where you might be able to find the lost ark. We'll explore what to live for and what to die for, and the difference between a nose job and a tattoo. Finally, we'll find out what the Fifth Amendment and Maimonides have in common.

I. Is G-d in the Bedroom?

A. Defining the Religious Ideal

Learning Interaction 1

Which of these statements best represents the Jewish attitude toward sexual intimacy?

a.   It is allowed in the context of marriage as a necessary concession to human nature.

b.   It is justified because it enables the noble goal of procreation.

c.   It can be a positive, even holy, experience.

d.   It can be the ultimate vehicle for God's expression.

Text 1

Celibacy: The state of being unmarried and, therefore, sexually abstinent, usually in association with the role of a religious official or devotee. In its narrow sense, the term is applied only to those for whom the unmarried state is the result of a sacred vow, act of renunciation, or religious conviction. Celibacy has existed in one form or another throughout history and in virtually all the major religions of the world.

Encyclopædia Britannica Online, s.v. "celibacy"

Question for Discussion

Why does celibacy qualify as a generic spiritual and religious ideal?

Text 2

דע כי חבור זה הוא ענין קדוש ונקי כשיהיה הדבר כפי מה שראוי, ובזמן הראוי,
ובכוונה הנכונה. ואל יחשוב אדם כי בחבור הראוי יש גנאי וכיעור חס ושלום . . .
כל בעלי התורה מאמינים שהשם ברא את הכל כפי מה שגזרה חכמתו, ולא ברא
דבר שיהיה גנאי או כיעור . . . אלא פעולותיו של הקדוש ברוך הוא תמימות, שנאמר
(דברים לב,ד) "הצור תמים פעלו". ואומר (בראשית א,לא), "וירא אלקים את כל
אשר עשה והנה טוב מאד".

אגרת הקודש להרמב"ן, פרק ב

Know that sexual intimacy, when experienced in the proper time and with a proper state of mind, is pure and holy. One should not assume that it is obscene and shameful. . . .

Those familiar with the teachings of the Torah believe that God created everything in accordance with His wisdom and that He did not create anything obscene or shameful. His creations are flawless, as it says (Deuteronomy 32:4), "The deeds of the Rock are perfect." And it says, (Genesis 1:31) "And God saw all that He had made, and behold it was very good."

Rabbi Moshe ben Nachman, *Igeret Hakodesh* 2

Rabbi Moshe ben Nachman
(Nachmanides/Ramban, 1194–1270).
Scholar, philosopher, author, and physician. Nachmanides was born in Spain and served as leader of Iberian Jewry. In 1263, he was summoned by King James of Aragon to a public disputation with Pablo Cristiani, a Jewish apostate. Though Nachmanides was the clear victor of the debate, he had to flee Spain because of resulting persecution. He moved to Israel and helped reestablish communal life in Jerusalem. His classic commentary on the Pentateuch is printed in most editions of the Torah. He also authored numerous other works, including a commentary on the Talmud.

B. A Microcosmic Temple

Text 3

Babylonian Talmud. A literary work of monumental proportions that draws upon the legal, spiritual, intellectual, ethical, and historical traditions of Judaism. The 37 tractates of the Babylonian Talmud contain the teachings of the Jewish sages from the period after the destruction of the 2nd Temple through the 5th century CE. It has served as the primary vehicle for the transmission of the Oral Law and the education of Jews over the centuries; it is the entry point for all subsequent legal, ethical, and theological Jewish scholarship.

בשעה שהיו ישראל עולין לרגל, מגללין להם את הפרוכת ומראין להם את הכרובים
שהיו מעורים זה בזה, ואומרים להן: "ראו חבתכם לפני המקום כחבת זכר ונקבה".
תלמוד בבלי, יומא נד,א

When the Jews came up [to Jerusalem] for the festivals, they would roll aside the curtain [that separated the people from the Holy of Holies], and the cherubim—whose bodies were intertwined one with another—were shown to them. And the assembled Jews would be told, "Look! You are beloved before God as the love between man and woman."

Talmud, Yoma 54a

Question for Discussion

How does this text shed light on the Talmudic view regarding sexual intimacy?

Text 4 📜

ענין החבור הזה ענין עילוי גדול כשיהיה כפי הראוי. והסוד הגדול הזה סוד גדול
בכרובים שהיו מעורים זה בזה דמיון זכר ונקבה.
ואילו היה הדבר גנאי, לא היה מצוה רבונו של עולם לעשות ככה ולשום אותם
במקום היותר קדוש וטהור שבכל הישוב.
אגרת הקודש להרמב״ן, פרק ב

Intimacy, when properly experienced, is great and sublime. It shares the profound secret of the cherubim, which were in the form of a male and female intertwined with each other.

If sexual intimacy were shameful, God would not have commanded to fashion the cherubim and place them in the holiest and purest place in the world!

Rabbi Moshe ben Nachman, *Igeret Hakodesh 2*

Text 5 📜

איש ואשה, זכו, שכינה ביניהן.
תלמוד בבלי, סוטה יז,א

When a husband and wife are worthy, God resides between them.

Talmud, Sotah 17a

Figure 3.1

אִישׁ אִשָּׁה

Text 6

כתיב (איוב כג,יג), "והוא באחד . . .".

"באחד"? "אחד" מבעי ליה! אלא במאן דאתתקן בקדושה עלאה למהוי חד, כדין הוא שריא באחד ולא באתר אחרא.

ואימתי אקרי בר נש אחד . . . בזמנא דאשתכח בר נש בזווגא . . . וכד מתחברן דכר ונוקבא כדין אתעבידו חד גופא, אשתכח דאינהו חד נפשא וחד גופא ואקרי בר נש אחד, כדין קודשא בריך הוא שארי באחד.

זוהר ג, פ,א–ב

Zohar. The seminal work of Kabbalah, Jewish mysticism. It is a mystical commentary on the Torah, written in Aramaic and Hebrew. According to Arizal, the Zohar consists of the teachings of Rabbi Shimon bar Yocha'i who lived in Israel during the 2nd century CE. The Zohar has become one of the indispensable texts of traditional Judaism, alongside and nearly equal in stature to the Mishnah and Talmud.

t is written (Job 23:13): "He is in one. . . ."

"[He is] *in* one"? Should it not read, "[He] *is* one"? [The meaning of this verse is that] God only abides and dwells "in one," in the person who achieves a holy oneness—nowhere else.

When is a person called "one"? . . . When a person is in the union of intimacy. . . . When male and female join, they become one. They are one in body and one in soul; they are one person. And God dwells in the oneness.

Zohar 3:80a–b

---

84   fascinating facts

C. Achieving Oneness

Text 7 🔖

שלא ינהג בה מנהג פרסיים, שמשמשין מטותיהן בלבושיהן . . . האומר, "אי אפשי
אלא אני בבגדי והיא בבגדה"—יוציא.

תלמוד בבלי, כתובות מח,א

A husband may not treat [his wife] in the manner of the Persians, who have marital intercourse while clothed. . . . Saying, "I can only [perform] while I wear my clothes and my wife wears hers," is grounds for divorce.

Talmud, Ketubot 48a

II. Who Shall Live?

A. Perfect Harmony

Learning Interaction 2

Based on your impression and/or knowledge of Jewish beliefs, in a case of conflict, which takes precedence: God's word (the *mitzvot*), or human life?

a.   God's word

b.   Human life

c.   I don't know.

Text 8

כשיעמוד גוי ויאנוס את ישראל לעבור על אחת מכל מצות האמורות בתורה או
יהרגנו, יעבור ואל יהרג. שנאמר במצות (ויקרא יח,ה), "אשר יעשה אותם האדם וחי
בהם"—וחי בהם, ולא שימות בהם.

משנה תורה, הלכות יסודי התורה ה,א

Rabbi Moshe ben Maimon
(Maimonides/Rambam, 1135–1204).
Halachic authority, philosopher, author,
and physician. Maimonides was born
in Cordoba, Spain. After the conquest
of Cordoba by the Almohads, he fled
Spain and eventually settled in Cairo,
Egypt. There, he became the leader of
the Jewish community and served as
court physician to the vizier of Egypt. He
is most noted for authoring the *Mishneh
Torah*, an encyclopedic arrangement of
Jewish law, and for his philosophical
work, *Guide for the Perplexed*. His rulings
on Jewish law are considered integral to
the formation of halachic consensus.

If a Gentile attempts to force a Jew to violate one of the Torah's commandments on pain of death, the Jew should violate the commandment rather than be killed, because it is stated concerning the *mitzvot* (Leviticus 18:5): "A person shall perform them and live by them." One should live by them and not die because of them.

Maimonides, *Mishneh Torah*, Laws of the Fundamentals of the Torah 5:1

B. Your Integrity or Your Life!

Learning Interaction 3

A man who won't die for something is not fit to live. ... I submit to you that if a man hasn't discovered something that he will die for, he isn't fit to live.

Dr. Martin Luther King, Jr., June 23, 1963

1. Do you agree or disagree with Dr. King's assertion?

2. Patrick Henry famously proclaimed, "Give me Liberty, or Give me Death!" He undoubtedly felt that life devoid of basic liberties was not worth living. Are there any lines in the sand that, if crossed, would render your life meaningless?

a. _____

b. _____

c. _____

Text 9

במה דברים אמורים? בשאר מצות, חוץ מעבודת כוכבים, וגלוי עריות, ושפיכת דמים. אבל שלש עבירות אלו, אם יאמר לו, "עבור על אחת מהן או תהרג"—יהרג ואל יעבור.

משנה תורה, הלכות יסודי התורה ה,ב

The above rule applies to all *mitzvot* with the exceptions of idolatry, forbidden sexual relations, and murder. With regard to these three sins, if one is ordered: "Transgress one of them or be killed," one should allow one's life to be taken rather than transgress.

Maimonides, *Mishneh Torah*, Laws of the Fundamentals of the Torah 5:2

Question for Discussion

Why are these three singled out as exceptions to the rule?

Text 10

Rabbi Samson Raphael Hirsch (1808–1888). Born in Hamburg, Germany; rabbi and educator; intellectual founder of the *Torah Im Derech Eretz* school of Orthodox Judaism, which advocates combining Torah with secular education. Beginning in 1830, Hirsch served as chief rabbi in several prominent German cities. During this period he wrote his *Nineteen Letters on Judaism*, under the pseudonym of Ben Uziel. His work helped preserve traditional Judaism during the era of the German Enlightenment. He is buried in Frankfurt am Main.

The only exceptions to the rule [that preserving life trumps mitzvah observance] are the prohibitions against idolatry, murder, and forbidden sexual relations. These are never preempted, even at the risk of death, for they represent the epitome of *mitzvot* between man and God, *mitzvot* between man and his fellow man, and personal sanctity.

Rabbi Samson Raphael Hirsch, Leviticus 18:5

fascinating facts

III. Bodily Affairs

A. Body on Loan

Text 11

No person shall be held to answer for a capital, or otherwise infamous crime, unless on a presentment or indictment of a grand jury, except in cases arising in the land or naval forces, or in the militia, when in actual service in time of war or public danger; *nor shall any person be subject for the same offense to be twice put in jeopardy of life or limb*; nor shall be compelled in any criminal case to be a witness against himself, nor be deprived of life, liberty, or property, without due process of law; nor shall private property be taken for public use, without just compensation.

Fifth Amendment, United States Constitution

Learning Interaction 4

What is your opinion regarding the "Miranda rights"?

a.   It sufficiently protects the accused.

b.   It does not go far enough in protecting the accused.

c.   It goes too far in protecting the accused.

Text 12

גזירת הכתוב היא שאין ממיתין בית דין ולא מלקין את האדם בהודאת פיו . . . שמא
נטרפה דעתו בדבר זה. שמא מן העמלין מרי נפש הוא המחכים למות, שתוקעין
החרבות בבטנם, ומשליכין עצמן מעל הגגות. שמא כך זה יבא ויאמר דבר שלא עשה
כדי שיהרג. וכללו של דבר גזירת מלך היא.

משנה תורה, הלכות סנהדרין יח,ו

I t is by decree of scripture that a court can execute neither capital nor physical punishment based on a person's own confession. . . . Perhaps this person's mind is crazed concerning this matter. Perhaps this person is one of those who are perturbed and embittered, who are anxious to die, who pierce their bodies with swords, or throw themselves from rooftops. We fear that, in order to be executed, such a person may come and confess to a crime that he did not commit.

Whatever the reason may be, this principle is a decree of the King.

Maimonides, *Mishneh Torah*, Laws of the Judiciary 18:6

Text 13

לפי שאין נפשו של אדם קנינו, אלא קנין הקדוש ברוך הוא, שנאמר (יחזקאל יח,ד),
"הנפשות לי הנה".
הילכך לא תועיל הודאתו בדבר שאינו שלו . . . אבל ממונו הוא שלו. ומשום הכי
אמרינן, "הודאת בעל דין כמאה עדים דמי" (גיטין מ,ב).
רדב"ז, שם

A person's life is not his own possession, but God's possession, for it is stated, "The lives are mine" (Ezekiel 18:4). Hence, confession [to a crime that will result in bodily harm] is null and void, because it concerns something that belongs to another.

Property, however, does belong to its owner. Hence, [concerning monetary issues] the Talmud (Gitin 40b) says, "A defendant's confession equals the testimony of one hundred witnesses."

Rabbi David ben Shlomo ibn Zimra, ad loc.

Rabbi David ben Shlomo ibn Zimra (Radvaz, 1479–1573). Born in Spain, he immigrated to Safed, Israel, upon the expulsion of the Jews from Spain in 1492. In 1513, he moved to Egypt and served as rabbi, judge, and head of the yeshivah in Cairo. He also ran many successful business ventures and was independently wealthy. In 1553, he returned to Safed, where he would later be buried. He authored what would later become a classic commentary to Maimonides' code of law, and wrote many halachic responsa, of which more than 10,000 are still extant.

B. Elective Plastic Surgery

Text 14

אסור לאדם לחבול בין בעצמו בין בחבירו, ולא החובל בלבד אלא כל המכה . . . דרך נציון הרי זה עובר בלא תעשה.

משנה תורה, הלכות חובל ומזיק ה,א

It is forbidden for a person to injure himself or another. Not only a person who causes an injury, but anyone who strikes another person . . . with malice violates a biblical prohibition.

Maimonides, *Mishneh Torah*, Laws of Injury and Damages 5:1

Question for Discussion

How is this passage from Maimonides' code instructive with regard to the issue of plastic surgery?

C. Tattoos

Text 15a

וְשֶׂרֶט לָנֶפֶשׁ לֹא תִתְּנוּ בִּבְשַׂרְכֶם, וּכְתֹבֶת קַעֲקַע לֹא תִתְּנוּ בָּכֶם, אֲנִי ה׳.

ויקרא יט,כח

Y ou shall not make cuts in your flesh for a person [who died]. You shall not etch a tattoo on yourselves. I am the Lord.

Leviticus 19:28

Text 15b

שהיה מנהג הגוים שרושמים עצמם לעבודה זרה שלהם, כלומר שהוא עבד נמכר לה ומורשם לעבודתה.

ספר החינוך, מצוה רנג

I t was the custom of the heathens to brand themselves for their deity, thereby demonstrating that they are servants branded for its service.

Sefer Hachinuch, Mitzvah 253

Sefer Hachinuch is a work on the 613 commandments, arranged in the order of each *mitzvah's* appearance in the Torah. Four aspects of every mitzvah are discussed in this work: the definition of the mitzvah and its sources in the Written and Oral Torah; ethical lessons that can be deduced from the mitzvah; basic laws pertaining to the observance of the mitzvah; and who is obligated to perform the mitzvah and when. The work was composed in the 13th century by an anonymous author who refers to himself in the introduction as "the Levite of Barcelona." It has been widely thought that this referred to Rabbi Aharon Halevi of Barcelona (Re'ah); however, this view has been contested.

Lesson Summary

1. While there are commonalities to be found in all religions, including such ideas as purpose and living a spiritually conscious life, there are many areas in which the Jewish perspective is quite distinct and unique.

2. Conventional religious wisdom views spirituality as a contradiction to the body, human love, married life, and sexuality. Judaism views things very differently. The ideal is that all our physical endeavors—dating, intimacy, children, career—should be a meaningful G-dly experience.

3. It is inconceivable that God would imbue every human being with an innate drive that is inherently and completely evil. When experienced properly, marital intimacy is a positive, even holy, endeavor.

4. There is a correlation between the cherubim, which were in the Holy of Holies, and marital intimacy. According to Kabbalah, the most optimal vehicle for a manifestation of G-dliness is the unity of male and female.

5. Judaism extols the virtues of marital relations only when it is within the context of a loving marriage and only when it expresses cognitive, emotional, and spiritual oneness.

6. Human life takes precedence over mitzvah observance because the *mitzvot* were given for the benefit of the Jewish people. Violating a Torah precept when a life is in danger is not a concession or compromise. One should not try to pass on the task or do it with reluctance and halfheartedness.

7. If a Jew is asked to murder, worship idols, or perform sexually prohibited acts, he should give up his life rather than do so.

8. According to Jewish law, self-incrimination is never allowed in criminal cases. Thus, torture to extract a false confession was never an issue in Jewish law inasmuch as the extracted confession would have been null and void anyway.

9. A person's body is not his own property; rather it belongs to God. For this reason, it is forbidden to harm oneself in any way. This is an area in which Judaism clearly diverges from the contemporary Western value of personal autonomy.

10. The preponderance of halachic opinions permit elective plastic surgery when there is a deformity—whether congenital or acquired—that, if uncorrected, would cause the person psychological anguish.

11. Tattooing one's body is forbidden in Judaism; however, there is no truth to the idea that a person with a tattoo cannot be buried in a Jewish cemetery.

Appendix

Learning Interaction

Circle the answer you find most accurate.

Satan is:

a.   the archenemy of God.

b.   a fallen angel who sinned and was punished.

c.   a devoted angel who is doing exactly what he is meant to do.

d.   nonexistent in the Jewish tradition.

Additional Readings

Judaism and Cosmetic Surgery

by **Daniel Eisenberg, M.D.**

The first successful partial face transplant from a donor was performed November 27, 2005 in Amiens, France. The recipient had lost her nose, lips, and chin after being mauled by her dog. The injuries left her grotesquely deformed, making it virtually impossible for her to interact normally with others. Muscles, blood vessels, nerves, and other tissues were transplanted from a "brain dead" donor in order to fashion a "hybrid" face that neither resembled the donor nor the recipient's original face. Since that time, several more face transplants have been performed, including a near total face transplant at the Cleveland Clinic in December, 2008.

These surgical procedures marked a new milestone in transplantation, adding new questions to the usual list of ethical issues involved in transplantation. Unlike kidney, liver, lung, or other vital organ transplants, which are life-saving procedures, the recent face transplants bring transplantation into the realm of plastic surgery.

From a Jewish perspective, the face transplant raises two sets of questions. There are the technical questions regarding transplant[1] and a more fundamental set regarding the approach of Judaism to vanity and plastic surgery.

Let us leave aside the issues of cadaveric transplantation and brain death involved in the recent face transplant cases and ask the more basic question of how far an individual may go to improve his/her appearance? Clearly the face transplant patients' surgeries were not prompted by mere vanity, as these patients were horribly disfigured. But, we must still ask if even routine plastic/cosmetic surgery is permitted at all? What are the possible concerns that may arise for one contemplating plastic surgery?

Cosmetic versus Reconstructive Surgery

Plastic surgery may be divided into cosmetic and reconstructive surgery. The former is performed for enhancement of one's physical appearance (such as rhinoplasty, liposuction, or breast augmentation). The latter is performed to correct a defect, whether congenital (from birth) or acquired (suffered in a car accident, for instance). These two indications for surgery may overlap and there is not necessarily a clean line that separates deformity from normal appearance. As has often been repeated, beauty is in the eye of the beholder.

Judaism treats the subjective sense of the individual very seriously when a person feels unattractive. What about a self-perceived cosmetic defect, one that is neither a true congenital defect nor the result of an injury? How much importance does Judaism place on self-esteem and self-consciousness?

The History of Plastic Surgery

The oldest descriptions of plastic surgery date back to 2600-year-old Sanskrit texts and ancient Egyptian papyri. These documents describe nose, ear, and lip reconstructions utilizing surgical flaps and skin grafts. Nevertheless, the term "plastic surgery" to describe reconstructive surgery was not introduced until 1818.[2]

Despite the long history of plastic surgery, no responsa were written about surgery performed for cosmetic surgery until the latter half of the 20th century. This is hardly surprising, since prior to the mid 19th century, all surgery was limited by the inability to adequately

---

[1] See Eisenberg, D, "Organ and Tissue Donation," JME, Vol. VI, No. 2 (Oct. 2008).

[2] http://www.emedicine.com/plastic/topic433.htm

ameliorate the pain of the surgery itself and the high morbidity and mortality of surgery in general.

This all changed due to important advances made in the second half of the 19th century. Building upon the work of Ignaz Philipp Semmelweis (who argued that hand washing would decrease hospital infections) and Louis Pasteur (who proved that bacteria cause infection), Joseph Lister introduced the concept of antiseptic surgery in the late 19th century, significantly decreasing the risk of surgical infection. Ether, the first form of general anesthesia, was publicly utilized for the first time on October 16, 1846, in an operating theater at the Massachusetts General Hospital, ushering in the age of modern anesthesia.[3] With these two breakthroughs came rapid advances in surgical techniques, and advancements in both reconstructive and cosmetic surgery, particularly between the first and second world wars.

The contemporary era of plastic surgery was ushered in by World War I. Due to the nature of trench warfare, which protected the soldier's lower body but exposed the head and neck to destructive new explosive devices, thousands of soldiers returned from war with horrible facial deformities. In order to aid these soldiers to integrate back into society, where they were finding difficulty finding jobs and spouses, several countries, including the United States, created special medical programs and hospitals dedicated to treating these injuries. World War II led to further advances in cosmetic surgery, largely for the same reason.[4]

As Max Thorek (the founder of the International College of Surgeons) pointed out, even modern cosmetic surgery was the direct result of war:

"If soldiers whose faces had been torn away by bursting shells on the battlefield could come back into an almost normal life with new faces created by the wizardry of the new science of plastic surgery, why couldn't women whose faces had been ravaged by nothing more explosive

than the hand of the years find again the firm clear contours of youth."[5]

Thus was born the era of widespread "plastic" surgery.

The Earliest Responsum

As plastic surgery developed and the options for cosmetic enhancement grew, formal halachic discussion began. In 1961, Rabbi Immanuel Jakobovits, considered by many to be the father of the discipline of Jewish medical ethics,[6] addressed the American Society of Facial Plastic Surgery at a symposium entitled "Religious Views on Cosmetic Surgery."[7] Rabbi Jakobovits, later Chief Rabbi of Great Britain, discussed the parameters of plastic surgery from a Jewish legal perspective.

After explaining that no responsa had yet been written on the topic, he dealt with the question of whether one may undergo plastic surgery for the purpose of improving one's physical appearance. As Rabbi Jakobovits

---

[3] http://www.etherdome.org/Our_Stor/Our_Stor.html

[4] Backstein, R and Hinek, A, War and Medicine: The Origins of Plastic Surgery, University of Toronto Medical Journal, vol. 82, no. 3, (May 2005)

[5] Tackla M. Phoenix from the flames: plastic surgery emerges out of the horrors of World War I. Cosmetic Surgery Times. Oct. 1, 2003. Cited by Backstein and Hinek, ibid.

[6] Rabbi Jakobovits is considered by many to be the father of modern Jewish medical ethics as a specialized area of study, due to the publication in 1959 of his doctoral thesis in book form, entitled "Jewish Medical Ethics." For the first time, the breadth of Jewish attitudes toward crucial medical issues was available to the general public and healthcare workers in readable English. As Dr. Fred Rosner describes it:

"Rabbi Jakobovits' now classic book is the first comprehensive treatise on the subject of Jewish medical ethics. Tracing the development of Jewish and other religions' views on medico-moral problems from antiquity to the present day, the book is profusely annotated by references to the original sources in religious, medical, legal and historical literatures. The book contains discussions of classic subjects in Jewish medical ethics such as abortion, artificial insemination, birth control, euthanasia, autopsies, eugenics, sterilization, treatment of patients on the Sabbath, and more. In addition, several chapters are devoted to the physician in Jewish religious law—his studies and privileges, his license and legal responsibilities, his professional charges and the admission of his evidence. The book is appropriately subtitled 'A comparative and historical study of the Jewish religious attitude to medicine and its practice.'" (Rosner, F, "Lord Immanuel Jakobovits: Grandfather of Jewish Medical Ethics," IMAJ 2001;3:304)

In 1981, Rabbi Jakobovits was knighted by Queen Elizabeth for his life of dedication.

[7] Published in The Eye, Ear, Nose and Throat Monthly, New York, Feb/March 1962

eloquently described in his classic work, Jewish Medical Ethics:[8]

"The problem was considered under four headings: the theological implications of 'improving' God's work or 'flying in the face of Providence'; the possible risks to life involved in any operation; the Jewish objection to any mutilation of the body; and the ethical censure of human vanity, especially among males."

He concluded[9] definitively that plastic surgery for aesthetic enhancement is a form of arrogance and vanity (particularly for men) and is forbidden unless the patient meets certain criteria. He later wrote[10] as part of an overview of the Jewish approach to medicine:

"In the sparse rabbinic writings on the subject, these reservations could be discounted, provided the danger is minimal; and especially 1) if the operation is medically indicated, e.g. following an accident, or for grave psychological reasons; 2) if the correction of the deformity is designed to facilitate or maintain a happy marriage; or 3) if it will enable a person to play a constructive role in society and to earn a decent livelihood."

The four ethical concerns of Rabbi Jakobovits remained the pivotal issues in all future responsa and therefore bear further elucidation, as subsequent poskim have approached them in different ways.

Ethical Concerns

The first potential practical objection to plastic surgery is the Torah obligation to guard health[11] which might limit the surgical risks that one may accept as part of plastic surgery. In addition to the hazards associated with the surgery itself, anesthesia, particularly general anesthesia, presents a very small but real risk of death or incapacitation.

Beyond the blanket obligation to guard health, there is the particular prohibition of self-mutilation. Just as one may not injure someone else, one may not cause injury to oneself. The prohibition of injuring someone else is called *chavala* and is derived directly from the Biblical verse[12] that warns the court not to give a convicted criminal more lashes than legally mandated. The verse is interpreted to mean that if the court must not strike a criminal without justification, surely an ordinary individual may not strike or otherwise injure his neighbor.

The Talmud[13] discusses whether this prohibition applies to harming oneself, concluding that "one who injures himself even though it is forbidden, pays no damages. But if someone else injures him, they pay damages." Injuring oneself without a valid reason is called *chovel b'atzmo*. This proscription has limitations however. We are only barred from causing unnecessary injury to ourselves. The key question is what is considered necessary.

Risk and harming oneself are not the only issues. There are also philosophical considerations. Do we assert that God, as the ultimate craftsman Who fashions human beings, makes each person exactly as they should be and that our "remodeling" of ourselves is an affront to His judgment? That is, does the divine mandate to heal and obligation to seek medical treatment extend to plastic surgery?

The fourth issue applies predominantly to men. The Torah commands that a man not wear the clothing of a woman and that a woman not wear the clothing of a man.[14] This prohibition extends beyond mere clothing, but includes actions and activities that are characteristic of one of the sexes.[15] For instance, in most situations a man may not dye his white hairs back to black for purposes of improving his appearance since this is considered to be a feminine activity.[16] Is plastic surgery also considered a "feminine" activity?

---

[8] Jakobovits, Immanuel, Jewish Medical Ethics: A Comparative and Historical Study of the Jewish Religious Attitude to Medicine and its Practice, 2nd Edition, Bloch Publishing Company, New York, 1975, p. 284.

[9] Jakobovits, Immanuel, Noam 6:273 (Abridged in Sefer Assia 1:222-223).

[10] Jakobovits, Immanuel, "Medicine and Judaism: an overview," Assia (English) 1980 Nov; 7(3-4):57-78.

[11] Deuteronomy 4:9 & 4:15. See *Shulchan Aruch, Choshen Mishpat* 409:3 and 427:8.

[12] Deuteronomy 25:3

[13] *Baba Kama* 91b.

[14] Deuteronomy 22:5

[15] Shabbos 94b, Nazir 58b-59a, *Shulchan Aruch, Yoreh Deah* 182.

[16] Maimonides, *Mishneh Torah, Hilchos Ovdei Kochavim* 12:10

A Variety of Approaches

In 1964, Rabbi Mordechai Yaakov Breish, Rabbi Menasheh Klein, and Rabbi Moshe Feinstein were each asked to rule on questions of cosmetic surgery for enhancement of appearance.

Rabbi Mordechai Yaakov Breish (1895-1976), author of the Chelkas Yaakov and a prominent posek [authority in Jewish law] in Switzerland, discussed the issues of risk and *chavala* (self-injury) when asked whether a woman may undergo cosmetic surgery to straighten and decrease the size of her nose in order to improve her chance of finding a suitable husband.[17]

He used a previous ruling of Rabbi Abraham of Sochachev, the 19th century author of the Avnei Nezer, as a starting point for his discussion of why it is permitted to enter into surgery or other dangerous situations, even when not absolutely necessary. The Avnei Nezer[18] had forbidden a child to have surgery to straighten a crooked leg due to the risk of the operation. Rabbi Breish points out several objections to this ruling.

So long as a doctor practices in an acceptable way, it is a mitzvah for a physician to treat even non-life-threatening illnesses even though he may injure or kill patients inadvertently.[19] That is the nature of the mandate to heal. Additionally, the Talmud allowed bloodletting as a preventative health mechanism, even though it was known to be somewhat dangerous. We also clearly see that one is not prohibited from entering into a dangerous situation voluntarily since we do not prohibit women from having babies, despite the risks associated with pregnancy and childbirth.[20]

Rabbi Breish also points out that the general population undergoes surgery for non-life-threatening conditions with a very low complication rate. He therefore invokes the concept of *Shomer Pesaim Hashem*,[21] that God watches over the simple, to defend low risk surgeries. He rules that from the perspective of risk, one may pursue plastic surgery as it is one of the activities that the general population finds to be acceptably safe.[22] To support his contention that one may injure oneself (independent of any associated risk) for treatment of a non-life-threatening malady, he brings two proofs. The Code of Jewish Law[23] warns a child not to remove a thorn, bloodlet, or amputate a limb from a parent, even for medical reasons, lest he transgress the capital offense of injuring a parent. Rabbi Moshe Isserles, in his gloss to the Code of Jewish Law, states that the child should only refrain if there is someone else present who can help the parent, for otherwise, the child should even amputate the limb if the parent is in pain. It seems clear that the prohibition is only to injure one's parent *unnecessarily*. But, the concept of bloodletting or amputation of a parent's limb *per se,* merely to relieve pain, despite the trauma involved, does not appear to be problematic!

The second proof is fundamental to our discussion of plastic surgery, particularly cosmetic surgery. The Talmud[24] states that a man may remove scabs from his body to alleviate pain, but not to improve his appearance.[25] At first glance, this may appear to exclude the possibility of plastic surgery. However, Tosofos,[26] commenting on this statement, promulgates a concept that demonstrates a very sensitive understanding of human nature and psychology. He writes: "If the only pain that he suffers is that he is embarrassed to walk among

---

[17] *Chelkas Yaakov, Choshen Mishpat* 31

[18] *Avnei Nezer Yoreh Deah* 321

[19] Nachmanides, *Toras Ha'Adam, Inyan Ha'Sakana.* See also *Beis Yosef, Yoreh Deah* 241

[20] Women are not required by the Torah to have children.

[21] Psalms 116:6

[22] The Torah has several *mitzvos* regarding personal safety. For instance, we are instructed to build a parapet around any flat roof, to prevent anyone from falling (Deuteronomy 22:8). Maimonides (*Mishneh Torah, Hilchos Rotzeach* 11:4) explains this to include any dangerous situation, such as an unguarded swimming pool. We must be proactive in eliminating all preventable risks, such as covering ditches on one's property (*Shulchan Aruch Choshen Mishpat* 427:6-7).

In addition to removing hazards, the Torah twice commands us to protect our health, safety and well being (Deuteronomy 4:9 & 4:15). For example, the Talmud forbids walking near a shaky wall, lest it fall and injure the passerby. Similarly, all dangerous pursuits are proscribed. Obviously, there is latitude in evaluating how much risk is acceptable. The Talmud asks in several places (for example, *Shabbos* 129b) why certain potentially dangerous actions are permitted. It answers that a person need not avoid small risks that are accepted by the rest of normal society without undue concern. This concept is called "*Shomer pasaim Hashem, dashu bay rabim*"

[23] *Shulchan Aruch, Yoreh Deah* 241:3

[24] *Shabbos* 50b

[25] Rashi comments that for a man to remove scabs for aesthetic reasons is feminine behavior.

[26] *Shabbos* 50b, Opening phrase "*bishvil.*"

people then it is permissible, because there is no greater pain than this." Tosofos recognizes that there is no greater suffering than psychological pain and that it is very difficult to judge for someone else the degree of suffering they are experiencing as a result of a self-perceived defect.

Citing the psychological pain associated with the inability to find a spouse, Rabbi Breish ruled that the woman may have the cosmetic surgery.

That same year, Rabbi Moshe Feinstein (1895-1986) was asked the same question. His responsa first examines the parameters of the prohibition of *chavala*.[27] He points out that in his Mishneh Torah,[28] Maimonides clearly describes *chavala* as injury with malice. Rabbi Feinstein brings several examples of injury without the intention to do harm that Jewish religious literature finds acceptable.[29] His final ruling permits surgery when it is in the best interests of the patient, even if they are not sick and it does not treat an illness.[30] As a result, he permitted the woman to have cosmetic surgery since it was to her advantage and not being done to harm her.[31]

---

[27] *Igros Moshe, Choshen Mishpat* 2:66

[28] *Mishneh Torah, Chovel U'Mazik* 5:1. See *Shulchan Aruch, Choshen Mishpat* 420:31.

[29] The four examples listed by Rabbi Feinstein are:

a. In the book of Kings I 20:35-36, a man is punished for refusing to hit a prophet. A discussion of the event is also recorded in Sanhedrin 89.

b. *Baba Kama* 91b describes that Rav Chisda would lift up his garment when walking through thorn bushes so that his legs would be scratched, but his clothes would not be hurt. He reasoned that his legs will repair themselves, but his clothes would not.

c. *Sanhedrin 84b* discusses the permission to do bloodletting on one's father if necessary based on the mitzvah, "*V'ahavta l'reacha kamocha*" ("Love your neighbor as yourself"). Rabbi Feinstein explains that we learn that one may cause an injury to his friend which is of a type that a reasonable person would want to have done to them, e.g. bloodletting. The Talmud does not even imply that bloodletting itself is halachically problematic, only that one must be careful when doing it on a parent. Injury as part of medical treatment is permitted and is only considered *chavala* when the intent is to injure or disgrace someone.

d. *Mishna Bechoros* 45a discusses one who removes an extra digit from his hand without any indication that such surgery is forbidden.

[30] Nevertheless, see *Igros Moshe, Orach Chaim* 3:90 where Rabbi Feinstein argues that the Torah grants a mandate to heal only in cases of illness or injury, but not in order for a person to fulfill a mitzvah. Therefore, he rules that one may not have an intravenous line inserted before Yom Tov in order to allow fasting on Yom Kippur.

[31] Rabbi Feinstein (*Igros Moshe, Choshen* Mishpat 2:65) took the same approach when asked whether dieting for the sake of improving a woman's appearance alone is permissible since the Talmud (*Baba Kamma* 91b) teaches that *chovel b'atzmo* (injuring oneself) is forbidden and Tosofos explains that this is even if the injury is for a purpose. Rabbi Feinstein first explains that dieting for

Also in 1964, Rabbi Menasheh Klein, author of Mishneh Halachos, dealt with the question of the permissibility of cosmetic surgery to correct various facial imperfections that mar a woman's appearance, such as a very long nose which makes it difficult for her to marry and which she feels makes her very unattractive.[32] Rabbi Klein utilizes an ingenious approach to evaluate the question. He points out that there is ample precedent for medical intervention to improve appearance dating back to Talmudic times.

The Mishna[33] discusses the case of a man who betroths a woman on the condition that she has no defect (*mum*) where a "*mum*" is defined as any defect that would bar a Cohen (Jewish priest) from serving in the Temple. Tosofos[34] states that if the woman had her blemish corrected by a physician before her engagement, the marriage is valid. Since many of the blemishes that would apply to a Cohen include cosmetic imperfections[35] of the face for which people today would desire elective plastic surgery and Tosofos permits these blemishes to be corrected by a physician, Rabbi Klein states that it appears that a man or woman may go to a doctor to correct a cosmetic defect merely for enhancement of their appearance. Rabbi Klein rejects the argument that plastic surgery entails any danger whatsoever based on information he received from physicians.

In a second responsum,[36] printed immediately following the previously discussed one, Rabbi Klein discusses plastic surgery and chemical peels in men with respect to the prohibition of a man performing female behaviors. He reiterates his previous ruling and adds that (minor) cosmetic procedures are forbidden for men if done strictly for aesthetic enhancement, but that the

---

medical reasons is certainly permitted. He then argues that if the hunger caused by dieting would cause true pain (which Rabbi Feinstein questions), it would be forbidden to diet for cosmetic purposes. But, Rabbi Feinstein argues that the real pain that ensues from dieting is merely the pain of abstaining from desirable food, which is not true suffering. Therefore, he argues that we must compare the pain of dieting against the pain of feeling unattractive. If the woman's pain from abstaining from enjoyable food is less than the pain that she feels from her appearance, the diet is permitted.

[32] *Mishneh Halachos* 4:246

[33] *Kesubos* 72b

[34] *Kesubos* 74

[35] *Bechoros* and *Mishneh Torah, Be'as Hamikdash*, 8

[36] *Mishneh Halachos* 4:247

prohibition does not apply if the blemish causes the man enough embarrassment that he shuns social interaction. Rabbi Klein wisely points out that such a distinction requires a great deal of intellectual honesty.

In 1967, Rabbi Yitzchak Yaakov Weiss (1902-1989), head of the Eida Chareidis rabbinical court in Jerusalem and author of *Minchas Yitzchak*, dealt briefly with the issues of *chavala* and risk with respect to plastic surgery.[37] He takes the same approach to self-injury as Rabbi Feinstein, arguing that the prohibition of *chavala* only applies when the wound is inflicted with the intention of causing harm or degradation. He feels that cosmetic surgery would be permitted if not for the risk of surgery, which he believes to be a serious concern. He refers to one of his earlier responsa[38] which was directed to his in-law, Rabbi Breish, in which he forbids surgery for non-life-threatening conditions. While admitting that the line of reasoning of Rabbi Breish has merit, he disagrees, arguing that the permission of the Code of Jewish law to allow amputation of a limb is only in a life-threatening situation. He also agrees with Rabbi Breish that people desiring plastic surgery may be ill, but states that they are not endangered, and therefore is hesitant to allow elective plastic surgery, ending his 1967 responsa by saying the question requires further study.

Despite the generally strong support among halachic experts for the permissibility of reconstructive surgery for congenital defects and traumatic injuries, one dissenting opinion stands out with regard to cosmetic surgery merely to enhance one's appearance.

I am the Lord Your Healer[39]

There is an inherent tension in Judaism regarding the philosophical underpinnings of the mandate to heal. While the Torah clearly empowers the physician to treat illness, there is controversy regarding how far the permission extends.[40] While most Biblical commentators and Jewish legal scholars interpret the Torah to grant a very broad license to heal, there is a consensus that the patient must be ill to allow the physician to treat the patient, particularly if the treatment is dangerous or requires injuring the patient in the process of healing.

This is one of the major concerns voiced by Rabbi Eliezer Yehuda Waldenberg (1917-2006), author of *Tzitz Eliezer*, a multivolume set of responsa, much of which deals with medical issues. First, Rabbi Waldenberg[41] objects to performing surgery on someone who is neither sick nor in pain.[42] He argues that such activities are outside the boundaries of the physician's mandate to heal (since he questions whether cosmetic surgery is truly included in the category of healing). He further asserts that the patient has no right to ask the physician to wound him or her for the purposes of merely enhancing beauty. Rabbi Waldenberg then makes the theological argument that as the ultimate artisan, God creates each person in His image, exactly as he or she should be, with nothing extra nor anything lacking. He therefore posits that cosmetic surgery that is not pursued to relieve pain or true illness is an affront to God and is forbidden.[43]

[37] *Minchas Yitzchak* 6:105

[38] *Minchas Yitzchak* 1:28

[39] Exodus 15:26

[40] There is a great deal of controversy in Jewish halachic literature as to where we derive the mandate to heal. Depending on the origin of the permission to heal, a different set of parameters limiting medical treatment arise. While most

authorities derive a very broad mandate there are a few very famous minority opinions that severely limit the scope of the authorization to provide medical care. Ibn Ezra (in his commentary to Exodus 21:19) is a notable example, writing that the command to heal "is a sign that permission has been granted to physicians to heal blows and wounds that are externally visible. But, all internal illnesses are in God's hand to heal." The Ibn Ezra's case is not a hard one to make. The Torah itself instructs that if we listen carefully to the mitzvot of the Torah "then any of the diseases that I placed upon Egypt, I will not bring upon you, for I am God, your Healer" (Exodus 15:26). This verse implies that God does not need man to cure the afflictions that He creates. The Ibn Ezra argues that the meaning of this Torah passage is that because God acts as the (sole) healer of all illness, we will not need physicians. See Eisenberg,,D, "*The Mandate to Heal*," "http://www.aish.com/societyWork/work/The_Mandate_to_Heal.asp

[41] Responsa *Tzitz Eliezer*, 11:41

[42] See Responsa *Tzitz Eliezer*, 12:43 where Rabbi Waldenberg rules that truly elective surgery is never permitted.

[43] Rabbi Waldenberg's approach is based on the accepted concept that there is no inherent right for man to practice medicine, but that direct permission was required from the Torah which carefully circumscribes the limits of medical practice (see *Tosofos*, *Bava Kamma* 85a, opening word, "*sh'nitna*"). The duty to save one's fellow man is well grounded in the Torah and the restrictions are discussed at length in our codes of Jewish law. The complexity of the philosophical tension between God's control of health and the role of the human healer is encapsulated by the enigmatic opening words of the Code of Jewish Law's discussion of the laws applying to physicians: "The Torah gives permission to the physician to heal; moreover, this is a mitzvah and it is included in the mitzvah of saving a life; and, if he withholds his services, he is considered a shedder of blood." (*Shulchan Aruch, Yoreh Deah* 336)

Why is permission specifically granted here? Because only here we may have thought that the action should be forbidden. Left to our own logic, we would have no choice but to assume that God makes people sick and God alone heals (see note 40). But, once the Torah clearly stated that healing is permitted, it

A Final Argument

The last major posek to voice an opinion is a fitting conclusion to our discussion of the various approaches of Jewish legal authorities to plastic surgery. Dr. Abraham Abraham reports[44] the opinion of Rav Shlomo Zalman Auerbach (1910-1995), the great Israeli posek, on the question of a person whose arm or finger had been traumatically amputated.

In response to those who forbid plastic surgery, Rabbi Auerbach discussed the question of whether an amputated limb could be reattached by surgery requiring general anesthesia, even if the patient had already been treated so that he was no longer in danger his life. He ruled that the surgery would certainly be permitted on a weekday[45] "since the surgery would not be considered an injury but a repair and treatment to save the limb. Why then should it be forbidden for someone to undergo plastic surgery in order to look normal?" In a published responsa,[46] Rabbi Auerbach writes:

If the plastic surgery is done to prevent suffering and shame caused by a defect in his looks (for instance a nose which is very abnormal) this would be permitted based on the Tosafot and the Gemara, since the purpose is to remove a blemish. However if the only reason is for beauty, this is not permitted.

Rabbi Auerbach sums up the consensus of most legal experts in ruling that plastic surgery to allow someone to appear normal, and more importantly to view themselves as appearing normal is permitted. It is only when such surgery is performed merely for vanity that the rabbis have serious reservations. Clearly however, true reconstructive surgery and even surgery for an appearance that makes one feel embarrassed is not an issue of vanity. Such was clearly the case with the French face transplant recipient.

---

immediately becomes a mitzvah—a religious obligation—like all other mitzvos. Therefore, the Code of Jewish Law quite appropriately states that "The Torah gives permission to the physician to heal; moreover, this is a mitzvah."

[44] *Nishmat Avraham, Yoreh Deah*, p. 62, Mesorah Publications (English version)

[45] "On *Shabbat* or *Yom Tov* this would not be permitted since there was only *danger to a limb* and one could not set aside Torah law for this." Ibid.

[46] *Minchas Shlomo Tinyana* 86:3 quoted in *Nishmat Avraham*, ibid.

This leaves us with a very potent human message. We must always appreciate the self-constructed prisons in which some of our friends and acquaintances live and the empathy of our rabbis to their plight. Whether it is the torture of feeling unattractive or the feeling of hopelessness of a single friend who is losing hope that he/she will ever have a wife/husband and family, we must always look for ways to ease their pain.

Jewish Medical Ethics and Halacha 7, no.1 (Schlesinger Institute for Medical-Halachic Research, 2009):24-29.
(Also published on Dr. Eisenberg's website, www.jewishmedicalethics.com)
Reprinted with permission of the author and publisher

An Intimate View on Intimacy

by Rabbi Manis Friedman

Conventional wisdom says that sexuality is a natural instinct. It's a very common and innocent human activity, it's what happens between a man and a woman, it's what people do and all we need to do is relax and enjoy it, right?

It seems so simple. But if it were so simple, why do we need to be reminded over and over again that it's natural, it's innocent, it's pleasurable, it's what we do, it's what happens, relax and enjoy it? In fact, the media has bombarded us with that message for so long and in so many different ways with such ingenuity that you have to wonder why the message hasn't been accepted. Why are we still so uncomfortable, so unsure, so mystified by our own sexuality?

In the world that the Almighty created, there are three conditions. First, there is the secular, weekday, mundane condition—ordinary, common things that we possess. Second, there is the holy, Divine condition—so heavenly that we don't have these things at all. These two parts, so

---

far, are pretty easily accepted and understood. The difficult part is the third condition, the sacred. Although sacred means set aside and unavailable, the sacred is not totally unavailable. The sacred is that which is holier than the ordinary, but not so holy that we can't approach it at all. It's something in between what we have and what we cannot have.

Confused? Let's use a simple example. The Almighty grants us the blessing of children. So, we have children. Your children. My children. But when we say "my children," is that a possessive "my"? Do I own my children? The answer, of course, is no. They're not really mine. They don't belong to me. When I say "my wife," is that a possessive thing? Does "my husband" mean that which belongs to me? Of course not. And yet, we can use a term so familiar as "my" in referring to these things in life. That's the sanctity in life, and if we're not careful, in our arrogance, we can lay claim to things that will never belong to us and lose their sanctity.

So, where does sexuality fit in? By its very nature—not by divine decree, not by religious belief or dictate—sexuality belongs to the arena of the sacred. We experience it, but we cannot own it. We can go there, but we don't belong there. We can be sexual, but we cannot possess our own sexuality. The reason for it is very natural and very basic. To be intimate means to go into a place that is private, that is sacred, that is set aside. Sexuality means one person entering into the private, sacred part of another human being's existence.

You cannot own another person's intimacy. It's not available. Even if the person wants to give ownership. Can't do it. It's not sharable. It's one of those things in life that the Almighty gives us that we can never possess. I cannot possess my children. I cannot possess my spouse. I cannot possess my Creator. I can't even possess my life. I, certainly, cannot possess the other person's intrinsic, sacred and unsharable part.

Well, if it's that unavailable, if I can't possess it, then what connection, what relationship do I have with it?

This is the sanctity we can experience, but cannot own. And that is why the pleasure in intimate relations is more intense than any other pleasure. You can enjoy a good meal. You can enjoy good food, and it's great pleasure, but it's not the pleasure of sexuality because you possess the food. It's yours. You planted the vegetables, you grew them, you plucked them and you ate them. They're yours. There's no awe involved. The pleasure of sexuality is that it's a combination of having and not having. It's a combination of ordinary and other worldly at the same time. It's something that you are granted, but you cannot own and possess. And when you feel that combination, the pleasure of being in another person's intimate space while at the same time remembering that you don't belong there—it's not your place and can never be your place—that's what makes sexuality different.

The key word is familiarity. With the sacred, you cannot afford to become familiar. With the truly divine, there's no danger. It's out of your reach—forget about it. With the secular and mundane, well, you should become familiar. So where does familiarity breed contempt? Where is familiarity really destructive and unwelcome? In sanctity. If you become familiar, too familiar, with the intimacy of another person's life, whether physical, emotional or mental, then you've compromised the sanctity.

In our tell-all world, visualizing the destructiveness of familiarity might be difficult. But you don't call your parents by their first name... because that's too familiar. We don't use the Almighty's name in vain... because it's too familiar. And for our grandparents and our great-grandparents, intimate relations was a sacred thing not to be talked about... because that would be too familiar. The relationship between a husband and wife was restricted to behind closed doors. It was a sacred thing, something you don't squander, share, or even speak about. That's why our grandparents could not talk about their relationship. They weren't keeping secrets—they were keeping something sacred.

Today, human sexuality is something you're supposed to become familiar with. We claim to already be familiar with our sexuality and we are ashamed to admit that we are not. We've removed the sanctity, all because we thought our uptight parents were keeping a secret from us. The media continues to bombard us with these brilliant, subtle messages of the "naturalness" and "openness" of human sexuality, and it's not convincing us. Try as we might, we cannot ignore what our bubbes and zaides knew: the marriage bed is a sacred thing and the only way it works is when you treat it with sanctity.

Still need proof? Look at those same bubbes and zaides a little closer. Those two people, who have been married fifty, sixty, seventy years, are still a little bashful with each other. They still blush with each other. They still excite each other. That is human sexuality. That is sanctity. And that is the last word on intimacy.

Reprinted with permission of The Judaism Website, Chabad.org

"Full Frontal Feminism": The False Front

by **Chava Shapiro**

In one of my classes during my freshman year of college, the professor assigned a chapter from the book *Full Frontal Feminism: A Young Woman's Guide to Why Feminism Matters*. The chapter was titled, "Feminists Do it Better (And Other Sex Tips)." The basic idea: Once you get past all of the anti-sex nonsense that these religious right-wing maniacs are propagating, you'll be liberated, empowered and, subsequently, "great in bed."

The author begins by debunking the apparent myth that feminists are opposed to sex. ("I'm better in bed than you are," she begins, "and I have feminism to thank for it.") She goes on to explain that, while they represent two extremes of the spectrum, "abstinence-only education during the day and Girls Gone Wild commercials at night" essentially promote the same idea—that women can't make their own decisions about sex. Armed with this premise, she concludes that whether by telling girls that sex is sinful or by exploiting their bodies for entertainment, our society conspires to make sure that women don't "have a good time in bed."

Hold on. Rewind. Yes, we must reject the abstinence-only education model that tells young women they are worthless without their virginity. Yes, we must reject the Girls Gone Wild mentality that treats women's bodies like commodities. But where did this conclusion come from, this assertion that all we girls really want is to have fun (I'll forgo the song reference)? Obviously, women want to be intimate without feeling guilty, sinful, debased, or dehumanized... But for fun? Roller coasters are fun. Live concerts are fun. Water-skiing is fun. Far from empowering, the Sex-for-Fun campaign turns intimacy into something cheap, shallow, empty and entirely degrading. Of course, the sexual revolution is not a novel idea but an implacably entrenched one. Many young women today feel pressured by the societal expectation to have casual sex in much the same way that their mothers felt pressured by the societal expectation to stay a virgin until marriage. In fact, young girls are often treated as somewhat pathological for wanting to wait until marriage. Unfortunately, many parents actually add to the pressure by stressing their understanding of the inner-workings of the modern teenage relationship, justifying their passivity by shrugging and saying, "Well, they're gonna do it anyway." This idea that sex is "no big deal" is depressing and, frankly, dangerous. And not just because of STDs. Study after study shows that the more sexual experience that girls have as teenagers, the more prone they are to depression and suicide.

Yet there are also dangerous consequences of telling girls that sex is inherently sinful and that they are worthless without their virginity. Making girls feel shamed and punished doesn't exactly promote a healthy body image and self-esteem. This approach even has the opposite effect often times, leading girls to rebel violently against what they see as oppressive abstinence-only propaganda.

Sex is the single most powerful and pervasive force in human existence. As a Jewish woman, I am fascinated with the extent to which Judaism outright rejects the mainstream Christian view of sex as a sinful and shameful act. Even in the context of marriage, Christianity sees sex as a necessary compromise, mainly to prevent humanity from dying out. (Meaning, you're not necessarily going to hell, but it's far from the ideal.) Furthermore, most religions view sex as taboo, while there are pages and pages of Talmud throughout which our sages discuss intimacy in intricate detail, down to the nitty-gritty. These teachings go back over 1,500 years.

In most religions, asceticism is the ultimate path to spirituality, but Judaism teaches that divorcing ourselves from the physical world actually goes against our mission, which is to make this world a place for Godliness; only through engaging with the physical can we access the divine. So, it makes sense that Judaism teaches that through intimacy, the single-most physical human act, one can reach the height of holiness. Importantly, while this largely stems from the potential to create human life, the holiness of intimacy is not dependent on the possibility or intention for procreation. The relationship between a Jewish husband and wife is, in itself, sacred.

Yet the powerful nature of intimacy is most evident in the fact that, depending on its context, it can give one a taste of the highest of spiritual heights or the lowest spiritual depths. Intimacy can be a meaningful, uplifting, intensely personal experience or a depersonalized, careless, purely biological release. Sex is the most chaotic and unrestrained of human instincts, but its beauty is experienced most completely in the confines of discipline and precision. It's a remarkable paradox.

We live in a narcissistic world, a world obsessed with immediate pleasure and instant gratification. So much of what we do is intended to feed our egotistical, animalistic drives. But young women don't need to do too much self-searching in order to realize that we instinctively need meaning, love and commitment in relationships. It's just how we're wired, and no so-called feminist can convince us that being shallow pleasure-seekers is somehow liberating. It's time we start embracing real relationships and rejecting sex as a recreational sport. It's time we reclaim the true meaning of sexual liberation. It's time we start a new revolution.

Printed with permission of the author

The Sexual Component in Love and Marriage

by **Rabbi Maurice Lamm**

The Power of Sex

Sex is the most powerful, all-pervasive force in human experience. It may be intensely personal, meaningful, and creative at one moment, and depersonalized, meaningless, and careless the next. Much of its glory is that it can bring us as close as we may get in life to experiencing the mystery of our mortality, and because of this it is sanctified. Yet it can also be a blind, nearly irresistible force seeking wanton release on the biological level, and in this way its sanctity is perverted. Paradoxically, sex—the most chaotic, powerful, and untutored drive—can only be fully experienced when it includes an element of discipline and precision.

Theologian Helmut Thielicke postulates a theology of sex on the premise that not even an iron will can truly withstand its force. *En apotropus le arayot*, the Talmud teaches: "No one can guarantee another's sexual innocence." Long ago the Rabbis said, "The greater the man, the greater the desire," equating personal power and libidinal power. "The sexual attraction first engages the eyes," say the moralists, "and the only effective way to eliminate immorality is to avoid its grasp at every turn."

But temptation, in the form of magazines, books, and movies, is a multi-billion dollar industry and permeates our society. The abuse of human sexuality has reached the stomach-turning point, and there seems to be no way to avoid it—no exertion of universal wills, no permanent cover for the eyes. It is ironic that this situation should exist at a time when cults are multiplying, more people are praying, and atheists are being ridiculed into extinction. It seems we are at a time of religious boom and moral bust.

You may ask, "What else is new?" Haven't religious and ethical leaders throughout history decried society's lack of morality? Yes, but it is different today. Not because the sanctity of sex is violated in practice, not because television brings temptation into the family's inner sanctum, and not because sexual gratification is readily available. Today sexual morality is rejected as an ideal, modesty is scoffed at, and chastity is rejected as anachronistic. Worse, those who articulately uphold moral standards, modesty, and chastity are disappearing; their arguments appear irrelevant.

The Bible rejects one who does only "whatsoever is right in his own eyes" (Deuteronomy 12:8). Today, the philosophy that "man is the measure of all things" is not confined to one group, it is the heritage of our whole society. If we are to be the final arbiters of all value, it follows that whatever serves our needs is declared "good." "The good life" is a life devoted to sensual experience—tennis, water-skiing, the theater. These activities are not intrinsically wrong; but it is noteworthy that the most basic ethical term is so easily transferred to physical pleasure.

We have adopted an ideology of narcissism informed by situational ethics: if you have pleasure and mutual consent anything goes—as long as no one gets hurt. For example, what is disturbing is not the ethical merit of a particular abortion, but the rationale for wholesale abortions: "It's my body and I can do what I want with it." Similarly, there is hardly a trace of guilt to be found in those responsible for media presentations of what is now considered "old-fashioned" sexual immorality. No attempt is made to correct the situation—that's just the way it is. But worse is the accepted justification for casual sex or an adulterous affair: "It makes me happy."

Today contraception, not conception, is the focus of research. The sex act has effectively been separated from its fulfillment—one is play, the other pro-creation. In a day when coitus is no longer necessarily connected with reproduction or with responsibility, not many pregnancies are likely to survive both contraception and abortion.

Today there is no talk of standards, G-d's or society's. It seems sex is all right in every form—so long as it is not repressed, Freud forbid. We are faced with this question: What shall sex be used for now that it is no longer tied to that sacred, cosmically significant function of perpetuating the family, the faith, and the human race? Society's answer appears to be very simple: fun—and fun has no rules.

Judaism on Sexual Boundaries

There is no single term for "sex" in the Bible. The title for the list of the Bible's prohibited sexual offenses is *gilui arayot*, "uncovering the nakedness" (Leviticus 18:6ff), and Maimonides classifies these chapters of the law under the rubric of *Kedushah* (Sanctity). Although Jewish tradition does not treat sexual experience systematically, reference to it can be found in every one of the Five Books of Moses, in every book of the Prophets, and *Ketuvim*, the "Writings." Even the Talmud contains candid, sometimes explicit clinical analyses and intimate details that would make a Victorian blush. What emerges is a moral discipline that is strict, yet highly sensitive to the human condition; one that affirms the joyfulness of the sexual experience, but insists that it express itself in controlled circumstances; and one that never deprecates marriage and at every opportunity deplores monastic asceticism.

Judaism's philosophy of sexual experience, love, and marriage begins with the Bible's first recorded paragraphs describing Adam's relations with Eve. This philosophy has weathered every new fad and every radical style that boldly declared its doctrine to the world, from the celibacy of Augustine to the free love of Bertrand Russell. Judaism has focused its greatest minds on understanding G-d's law and nature's demands, and throughout its history has succeeded in elevating sex, sanctifying marriage, and firmly establishing the family as the primary unit of the community.

Traditional Judaism makes the following general propositions about sex and its place in human society:

1. Sexual relations may take place only between a man and a woman. This means that sex with an animal is considered a perversion, and intercourse with a member of one's own sex prohibited.

2. Sexual relations and marriage are not permitted with someone outside the circle of the Jewish people (mixed

marriage) or inside the circle of close relatives established by the Bible and the Sages (incest).

3. Sexual relations are a *mitzvah*, a religious duty, within a properly covenanted marriage in accordance with Jewish law. Outside of that covenant, premarital sexual relations are not condoned and extramarital relations are considered crimes.

4. Sexual relations within marriage must accord with the laws of family purity with respect to the wife's menstrual cycle.

Rabbi Akiva deduced these fundamental ideas from a single verse (Genesis 2:24): "Therefore shall a man leave his father and his mother and shall cleave unto his wife, and they shall be one flesh." By extension, "his father" also includes his father's wife, even if she is not his mother, and his "mother" is meant literally—to exclude incest. "And he shall cleave," but not to another male—to exclude homosexuality; "to his wife," not to his neighbor's wife—to exclude adultery; "And they shall be as one flesh," not to animals—to exclude buggery.

Seven Axioms for Sexual Conduct

These propositions are based largely on the following axioms that form the fundamental concepts of human sexuality in Judaism.

1. The Human Being Is Not an Animal

Simple observation teaches us that we have the genitalia of animals and participate in a similar sexual process. Why, then, can we not act like animals? It does seem to be nature's way. Indeed, Freudian psychology teaches us generally that we must see ourselves as we are, pleasure-seeking animals, and that we will not succeed in negating our essential animality except at the risk of neurosis. In the physical and psychological sense, then, human beings are considered to be fundamentally no more than animals.

Convinced of the truth of this specious reductionism—that we are nothing but animals—we begin to act that way without guilt, and even with gusto. There are no rules for beasts to follow other than blind obedience to

instincts, satisfaction of needs, and "doing what comes naturally." The consequences of this irresponsible behavior can be disastrous, resulting in broken homes, broken hearts, loneliness, children born out of wedlock, loveless marriages, and infidelity. Ecclesiastes (3:19) declares only in bitterness, "Man has no preeminence above a beast, for all is vanity." But if that is all we are, then the world, humanity, the soul, and all of life becomes meaningless and empty. We were created in the image of G-d, and Judaism does not permit us to squander our humanity. *Ha-neshamah lakh ve'ha-guf Pa'alakh* ("the soul is Yours [G-d's] and the body is Yours, too") is a cornerstone phrase of the *Yom Kippur* liturgy. At the wedding service, a blessing is recited to remind the bride and groom that the human being is created in G-d's image.

Despite the similarity of sexual anatomy and parallel reproductive processes, the essential humanity of our sexuality can be discerned in the very fabric of the physical act. If it is to be successful, the sexual act must be based on a sense of concern for the partner. Helmut Thielicke notes that "there is a two-way communication in the structure of the libido, for the prerequisite for the fulfillment of pleasure is that the other person gives himself to it, that he participates. . . . The other person should not be a passive object upon which one's own urge is simply 'abreacted.'" Without this communication, coitus is disguised autoeroticism. We cannot successfully follow the animal instinct and achieve release, but must be synchronized with our partner in order to satisfy ourselves.

This "synchrony" required of sexual partners reflects a unique factor that is fundamental to our understanding of the difference between animal sex and human sex: A man's curve of sexual excitement tends to rise sharply and fall precipitously, while a woman's may rise more slowly and taper off gradually. At first this may appear to be an imperfection, when compared to the easy harmony of animals. But perhaps this apparent incongruity is designed to prevent human beings from merely following the erotic impulse in blind animal fashion. To achieve genuine satisfaction, we are forced to express our humanity. Sex exposes us to failure and success, and in all this it confronts us with the theme of human communication instead of mere animal copulation. It is precisely this human need to correct the natural impulse that impels the thirteenth-century author of *Iggeret ha-Kodesh*, a document on the mystical significance of marriage, to give detailed advice to his son on preparing his wife for the sexual act and designing the proper erotic atmosphere.

This exception of the human being from the rule of instinct in the natural realm teaches us that we must exercise our essential humanity in the area of sexual relations as in all other critical areas of life. We must reasonably and intelligently choose a life partner, make proper human covenants, order our lives and our priorities, control our urges, and submit to a higher discipline: a *halakhah*, the law we were given by G-d. This is a law that we need in order to protect our love, both from other humans who act like animals, and from the internal animal that we sometimes allow to crouch at the door of our souls.

While some segments of society attempt to animalize our humanity, Judaism tries to humanize that which is called animal.

2. The Human Being Is Not an Angel.

If we are not animals—and thus not permitted to abuse our sexual gift—we are also not angels who may abstain from sex altogether. We must live according to a higher ethical and moral law as beings created in the image of G-d, but reality dictates that we are not, and will never become, angels.

Judaism therefore frowns on celibacy. As recorded in the Talmud, Ben Azzai (one scholar among the thousands recorded) chose to remain celibate in order to study Torah and was chastised severely. This is in stark contrast to the celibacy of the two founders of Christianity, Jesus and Paul, and the pronouncements against the institution of marriage (I Corinthians 6 and 7), which accept it only as a concession to human frailty. To wit, Paul: People should marry only " . . . if they cannot contain . . .; for it is better to marry than to burn" (I Cor. 7:9); and Matthew: "Be a eunuch for the sake of Heaven" (19:12); and John Calvin, at the beginning of the Protestant Reformation: Marriage is "a necessary remedy to keep us from plunging into unbridled lust." Reinhold Niebuhr considers the Christian development

of the family a triumph over the negative Christian attitude to sex and marriage.

Judaism posits that sex is a gift from G-d. How could such a gift be considered evil or sinful? Properly used in a legitimate framework, sex is to be viewed positively as joy and as *mitzvah*. The patriarchs marry, the kings marry, the *kohanim* marry, the prophets marry, and the Sages marry. Nowhere is there the slightest indication that sex or family interfered with their mission. The term used for Isaac's sexual relationship with his wife is *me'tzachek*, rejoicing (Genesis 26:8). The author of *Iggeret ha-Kodesh* writes: "Let a man not consider sexual union as something ugly or repulsive, for thereby we blaspheme G-d. Hands which write a Torah scroll are exalted and praiseworthy; hands which steal are ugly."

While the sexual act is considered good in the proper context, there were some ascetic pietists who viewed the sheer pleasure of even the legitimate act with some disdain. In the seventeenth century, Rabbi Hayyim Vital established the rule of Kabbalists: "He should sanctify himself at the time of intercourse so that he should derive no pleasure from it." However, the Seer of Lublin indicated that this applies before the act, as it is impossible to have no pleasure during the act. The Seer quotes Rabbi Elimelech of Lyzhansk, active in the eighteenth century, as saying that there is no benediction before performing the *mitzvah* of intercourse, "because it cannot be performed without an admixture of the 'evil' inclination." Nonetheless, while one should not seek pleasure from it, and while a full blessing may not be recited over it, the author concludes that we should thank G-d if we have received pleasure, so that we should not be guilty of using sacred things without proper acknowledgement.

Sex is not sin, and it does not need to be spiritualized. It must, however, be humanized, by affirming the reality of its power and attractiveness, rejoicing in its presence, using it as a blessing for the benefit and development of humankind, and abstaining from it when its Creator forbids it. A corollary of the two statements—that we are neither animals nor angels—may be that we have aspects of both. In this case, our humanity would consist of proper resolution of the tensions and contradictory demands made upon us by our dual nature.

3. Human Sexuality Is Clean and Neutral.

Judaism believes that sex is morally neutral. Libidinal energy is an ambivalent power, the effect of which depends on what the human being does with it. Sex does not even have the status of an intrinsic value, but can function as a means to express love and build family, or as random personal gratification. Sex is neither bestial nor sinful, neither sacrament nor abomination, and so may not be abused or discarded. It is not to be denigrated as a necessary concession to human weakness, nor is it to be worshipped as an idol.

Genesis (1:31) tells us that at the end of the creation, G-d saw everything that He made and that it was *tov me'od* (very good). Interpreting the verse, Rabbi Samuel ben Nahman said: "*Tov*, good—that is the *yetzer tov*, the good inclination; *tov me'od*, very good—that is the *yetzer ha-ra*, the evil inclination. But how can an admittedly evil inclination be considered good, let alone very good? Because without it, man would not care to build a home, he would neither marry nor beget children, nor would he pursue a livelihood."

Judaism does not believe that sex in itself is evil; it is the abuse of sex that is evil.

4. Sexuality Cannot Be Separated from Character.

If we agree that the sexual force is neutral and that its good or evil qualities depend on how we use it, we can begin to appreciate that our sexuality can never be separated from our total personality. Thus the way we handle our own sexuality is not primarily a matter of facts, but of values. Indeed, sex can be a revealing indication of character—is our partner a giver or taker, sensitive or gross, caring or selfish, religious or irreligious?

If sex were merely a matter of physiological function, it could be treated like a mechanical problem—get the best engine, use the best technique, and achieve the best result. If it doesn't work, trade it in. If this were the case, then sexual partners would be interchangeable, and society would function as a warehouse for suitable parts. This mechanical concept is analogous to prostitution, which is concerned solely with the biological function. It follows, therefore, that the more one's life is motivated by isolated instinct, the more one tends to polygamy and the less one seeks a single person with whom to share everlasting love.

The Jewish world view makes it clear that sex cannot be mechanically abstracted from the totality of human activity. Thus, the problems of premarital sex, adultery, and casual sex are really questions of values.

5. Human Sexuality Has Meaning Only in the Context of Relationship.

Perhaps our greatest fear is that our lives will be meaningless. If sex, the most powerful and sensitive area of our lives is to have meaning, it must be used as an expression of love or affection for another person. If we depersonalize the act by relating to another person only on a biological level, we dehumanize our partner and rob ourselves of our own integrity. To be successful, the act of sex requires the sensitive involvement of both partners. Noninvolvement results in a mechanical orgasm that is ultimately meaningless and demeaning.

If simply sleeping together would produce happiness, then the prostitute would be the happiest person in society. According to Helmut Thielicke, what is an ethical deficiency for the person who seeks the prostitute—the need for the physiological function rather than the person—is for the prostitute a positive element of moral self-defense. She saves her sense of self-worth by withholding her "self" during sex.

It is this distinction that determines whether the act is merely another sensation, or a true step toward relationship. It is becoming characteristic of our society that old as well as young people seek experiences rather than relationships, episodes rather than the continuous growth toward greater love. Ramban, in his commentary to the fundamental verse of love and marriage in Genesis (2:24), notes: "First one must cleave to his wife, and then they will become one flesh. There can be no true oneness of the flesh without first experiencing a cleaving together of the heart."

The later Rabbis analyze the specific commandment of *onah*, the *mitzvah* that requires the husband to care for his wife's conjugal needs. They ask whether the *mitzvah* requires only the object of the act (*cheftzah*), or the subjective involvement of the person in the performance (*gavra*). After finely dissecting the *mitzvah* and reducing it to its several legal components, they firmly maintain that the sex act ordained by the Bible as the right of the wife must be accompanied by closeness (*kiruv*), and joy (*simchah*). Both of these qualities require *gavra*, the involvement of the total personality, not merely a physical performance.

The sexual union of two people on a primitive, impersonal, casual, biological level is a gross misfortune. If it is by mutual consent, it is simply mutual exploitation. It has met the test of liberty in that it is not coerced, but it has failed the test of meaning, sensitivity, decency, and responsibility to the future.

6. Sexuality Has Value Only in a Permanent Relationship.

In the Jewish view, it is insufficient to affirm that the act must have meaning: it must also have value. For Judaism, value in human sexuality comes only when the relationship involves two people who have committed themselves to one another and have made that commitment in a binding covenant recognized by G-d and by society. The act of sexual union, the deepest personal statement that any human being can make, must be reserved for the moment of total oneness.

The sexual act is the first and most significant event of married life, and its force and beauty should not be compromised by sharing coitus in the expectation that some day a decision will be made to marry or not to marry. The act of sex is not only a declaration of present love, it is a covenantal statement of permanent commitment. It is only in this frame of reference that sexual congress is legitimate, because only then is it a religious act, a *de'var mitzvah*.

Love by itself is not a sufficient motivation for sexual expression; love that is authentic will want to reserve the ultimate act for the ultimate commitment. The test of a good marriage is not compatibility in bed, but compatibility in life. Given love and respect, sexual technique can be learned. Engaging in sex to "test it out" de-sanctifies the act. It is not a rehearsal for marriage, it is a rehearsal for divorce.

The Torah speaks of the sexual act as carnal knowledge, as in (Genesis 4:1) "Adam knew his wife Eve" (Gen. 4:1). *Ye'diah* is the most sublime human knowledge because it knows the mystery, the soul of the beloved. In the sexual act, knowledge comes not only from physical intimacy and harmony and oneness, but also from experiencing the very depths of passion and extremes of emotion emanating from the loved one. It is knowledge from the inside. All such knowledge has two aspects: We learn about the other person, and we also experience ourselves at the extreme of our potential. Perhaps that is why taboos surround both love and death. A taboo is designed to protect us where we are most vulnerable and most mysterious—as we generate life in the privacy of our room, and as we take leave of life.

The increasing freedom from sexual restraint in this post-Freudian era is testimony to the demystification of sex and the irretrievable loss of precious "knowledge." We can conjecture further that perhaps the use of the term *yada* (revealing knowledge) for the sex act is contingent upon the prior existence of hiddenness, mystery. This *he-alem*, (concealment) exists both on the biological level—the internality of the female genitalia—and the societal—the idea of modesty, *tze'niut*, and its use of clothing to cover the body. As society sheds its clothing, there is progressively less to "know" by means of sexual exploration. If the object of carnal knowledge is to know our self as well as our mate, then the demystification of sex adversely affects our self-knowledge as well.

7. Sexuality Needs to Be Sanctified.

If sexuality is that deepest personal statement, filled with ecstasy and informed by knowledge, it follows that even within marriage sex is not considered simply a legitimated biological function. The Torah motivated the Jew to sanctify sex within marriage, for sex as a part of daily routine threatens to become wearisome and a dread bore, and sometimes more divisive than supportive. The laws of "family purity," which require abstinence during and shortly following the menstrual period, place the sexual act in a special category.

On a basic level, sanctity means separating oneself consciously from immorality and illicit thoughts. Maimonides incorporates the laws of sexual morality in a section of *Kedushah* (the Book of Holiness), and states that the deliberate separation from the illicit is an act of self-transcendence that constitutes sanctification. Ramban goes beyond Maimonides in his comment on the verse in Leviticus "Be you holy" (19:2): "Sanctify yourself even with that permitted you" is a call to those who strive to a higher level of spirituality and sensitivity to separate themselves from gross acts and uncouth behavior, even that which is technically permitted, so as not to become *naval bi-re'shut ha-Torah*, "a knave within the realm of the Torah."

Kiddushin—which signifies sanctity and betrothal—leads inevitably to *nissuin*—nuptials, elevation. Thus sanctification raises the physiological act of sex onto a higher, more spiritual level. This understanding of sanctity as leading to elevation is implied in the suggestion of the Talmud that it is preferable for a pious scholar to perform the conjugal act on the Sabbath. Rashi explains, "It is the night of joy, of rest, and of bodily pleasure." Such an affirmation is descriptive of how the Sabbath invested even bodily joys such as wearing special clothes and eating special foods with a special significance, elevating them to the realm of sanctified physical pleasures.

Sanctity also implies mystery. The Holy of Holies of the Temple, its inner sanctum, was visited only once every year, and then only by the High Priest. In the imagination of the people, it was a subject of awe and mystery.

Our society has lost the sense of the sacred, and there is little mystery attached to sex. Its physiology and technique have become commonplace to children, and teenagers are already tired and bored veterans.

Judaism teaches that the erotic act has wide significance, and that this physical act operates transcendentally. The creation of family and the consecration of marriage are events of which Jews sing at the wedding feast, *she-ha-simchah bi-me'ono*, "There is joy in His [G-d's] abode."

There are two terms for the sexual act. The better known is that which is used in the Bible and Talmud, *bi'ah*, which means "a coming" as in "he came unto her." The second is a Kabbalistic term, *chibbur*, which means "joining." It is used in *Iggeret ha-Kodesh*, which is subtitled *Sefer Chibbur Adam ve Ishto*, "The Book of Joining of Man and His Wife." The word and concept are based on the mystical vision of the cherubim facing and embracing one another in spiritual mutuality. It also connotes the ideal of *ye'diah*, "knowledge from the inside." The Kabbalah considers knowledge and joining synonymous—true "knowledge" derives only from an interpenetrating and joining of the two bodies, the knower and the to-be-known.

Where *bi'ah* is simply descriptive of the physical position of the male, *chibbur* implies a coming together of equals. While rape or seduction must be referred to as *bi'ah*, *chibbur* implies a need for consent.

Chibbur also recalls the fundamental Jewish mystical drive of uniting and mending into oneness the fragmented world of "broken vessels." Genesis records the separation of the rib from ancient Adam, and *chibbur* refers to the rejoining of that rib to the side of Adam. Judaism strives for an understanding and an affirmation of the concept of *chibbur* in the context of *yichud*, the mutual love of husband and wife. The contemporary writer I. Lewald says: "In the consciousness of belonging together, in the sense of constancy, resides the sanctity, the beauty of matrimony, which helps us to endure pain more easily, to enjoy happiness doubly, and to give rise to the fullest and finest development of our nature."

The Jewish Way in Love and Marriage [New York: Jonathan David Publishers, 1991], 24–34
Reprinted with permission of the publisher

Lesson 4

Sunrise, Sunset
Exploring the Jewish Life Cycle

Introduction

Life is unpredictable, but it certainly is exciting. In this lesson, you will learn why a birthday is like a departing ship and what the Torah shares in common with poetry. You will find out how a dead body is like a Torah scroll and discover why and how one is married before marriage.

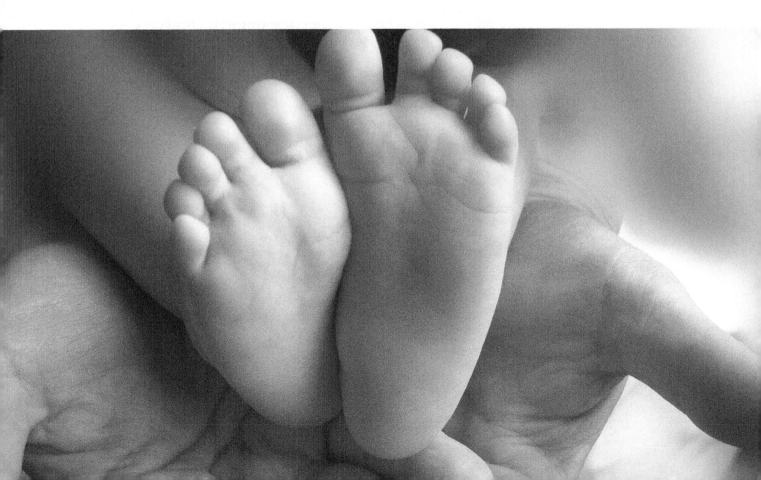

I. Happy Birthday!

Text **1a**

טוֹב שֵׁם מִשֶּׁמֶן טוֹב וְיוֹם הַמָּוֶת מִיּוֹם הִוָּלְדוֹ.

קהלת ז,א

A [good] name is better than good oil, and the day of death than the day of one's birth.

Ecclesiastes 7:1

Question for Discussion

How do you understand the message of this biblical verse?

Text **1b** 📖

נולד אדם הכל שמחין, מת הכל בוכין. ואינו כן, אלא נולד אדם ואין שמחין לו, שאין
יודעין באיזה פרק ומעשים יעמוד, אם צדיק ואם רשע, אם טוב ואם רע, ומת הם
צריכין לשמוח שנפטר בשם טוב ויצא מן העולם בשלום.
משל לשני ספינות פורשות לים הגדול, אחת יוצאת מן הלמן ואחת נכנסת ללמן
היוצאת מן הלמן הכל שמחין והנכנסת ללמן לא שמחו לה, היה שם פקח אחד אמר
להם חילוף הדברים אני רואה זו שהיתה יוצאה מן הלמן לא צריכין לשמוח עמה
שאין יודעין באיזה פרק עומדת כמה ימים מזדווגת לה כמה עלעולין הן מזדווגות,
ושנכנסת ללמן הכל צריכין לשמוח שנכנסה לשלום.
כך מת אדם, הכל צריכין לשמוח ולשבח שנפטר בשם טוב בשלום מן העולם. הוא
ששלמה אמר "ויום המות מיום הולדו".
מדרש, קהלת רבה ז,ד

When a person is born, all rejoice; when one
dies, all weep. However, it should not be
so. When a person is born, there should be
no rejoicing, because it is not known in what class he
will stand in terms of his actions, whether righteous or
wicked, good or bad. When he dies, however, there is
cause for rejoicing if he departs with a good name and
leaves the world in peace.

A parable: There were two ocean-going ships, one
leaving the harbor and the other entering it. As the one
sailed out of the harbor, all rejoiced; but no one displayed
any joy over the one that was entering the harbor. A
shrewd person was there and said to the people, "I take
the opposite view to yours. There is no cause to rejoice

over the ship that is leaving the harbor because nobody knows what will be its plight, what seas and storms it may encounter; but when it enters the harbor, all have occasion to rejoice because it has arrived safely." . . .

That is what King Solomon said, "And the day of death [is better] than the day of one's birth."

Midrash, *Kohelet Rabah* 7:4

Text 2

שהשמחה ביום הבר מצוה היא על יסוד הכלל בהלכה שכל ישראל בחזקת כשרות, היינו, שבודאי יקיים כל דיני התורה ומצוותיה [ובלשון הרמב"ם "מאחר שהוא מישראל . . . רוצה לעשות כל המצוות ולהתרחק מן העבירות" . . .] ולכן שמח ביום שזכה לחיוב במצוות.

ומזה מובן גם בנוגע להשמחה ביום ההולדת—היום שבו ירדה נשמתו לעולם כדי שיוכל לשמש את קונו על ידי קיום התורה ומצוות, ומצד חזקת כשרות בודאי יתנהג כן בפועל ממש, ובפרט כשהשמחה היא ביחד עם הוספה בתורה ומצוות, וקבלת החלטות טובות כו', היינו, שהחזקת כשרות באה לידי פועל ממש בהשמחה שביום ההולדת גופא.

ספר השיחות תשמ"ח ב, ע' 403–404

Celebrating a bar mitzvah joyously is premised upon the dictum in Jewish law that every person shall be regarded with a presumption of virtuosity. Thus, we assume that the person celebrating his bar mitzvah will certainly fulfill all of the Torah precepts and *mitzvot*. [Maimonides stated something similar, "A Jewish person . . . has an innate desire to fulfill all of the Torah's commandments." . . .] Therefore, one ought to be joyous on the day that one becomes obligated to perform the *mitzvot*.

Likewise, regarding the joy on a birthday—the day that the soul descended into this world to serve its Maker through the performance of Torah and *mitzvot*—because of the presumed virtuosity of every person, we must assume that this person will indeed fulfill his or her mission.

This is certainly the case if the birthday celebration is associated with an increase in Torah and *mitzvot* and adopting positive resolutions. In this way, the presumed virtuosity already manifests itself in actuality.

The Lubavitcher Rebbe, Rabbi Menachem Mendel Schneerson, *Sefer Hasichot 5748, 2:403–404*

Rabbi Menachem Mendel Schneerson (the Rebbe/Lubavitcher Rebbe, 1902–1994). Chasidic rebbe and the towering Jewish leader of the 20th century. Born in southern Ukraine, the Rebbe escaped Nazi-occupied Europe, arriving in the U.S. in June 1941. The Rebbe inspired and guided the revival of traditional Judaism after the European devastation, impacting virtually every Jewish community the world over. The Rebbe often emphasized that the performance of just one additional good deed could usher in the era of Mashiach. The Rebbe's scholarly talks and writings have been printed in more than 200 volumes.

Figure 4.1

- During the course of the day, make some "alone time" and think about the past year: what went right, what went not-so-right, and what can be fixed.

- Take your life to a new level with a new mitzvah.

- Give some extra charity.

- Spend more time in prayer. Take some extra time for Torah study. Share what you learn with friends.

- Every year of your life has a corresponding chapter in the Book of Psalms: your age +1 (that is, if you are turning thirty-two, your psalm is chapter 33). Recite your psalm today and continue to recite it each day for the coming year.

- Gather with friends and publicly thank God for the gift of life. This is an opportune time to encourage each other to strive for spiritual growth.

- Eat a new seasonal fruit on your birthday so that you can say the special *Shehecheyanu* blessing, thanking God for granting you life.

- For men: Arrange to receive an *aliyah* on the Shabbat before your birthday. If the Torah is read on your birthday, arrange to receive an *aliyah* on that day too.

II. Pregnancy

Text 3a

ומלמדין אותו כל התורה כולה. . . . וכיון שבא לאויר העולם, בא מלאך וסטרו על פיו,
ומשכחו כל התורה כולה.

תלמוד בבלי, נדה ל,ב

The fetus is taught the entire Torah.... As it enters this world, an angel approaches and slaps it on its mouth and causes it to forget the entire Torah.

Talmud, Nidah 30b

Babylonian Talmud. A literary work of monumental proportions that draws upon the legal, spiritual, intellectual, ethical, and historical traditions of Judaism. The 37 tractates of the Babylonian Talmud contain the teachings of the Jewish sages from the period after the destruction of the 2nd Temple through the 5th century CE. It has served as the primary vehicle for the transmission of the Oral Law and the education of Jews over the centuries; it is the entry point for all subsequent legal, ethical, and theological Jewish scholarship.

Text 3b

Why was it important to teach the fetus material it cannot possibly carry over into life? Why teach what will soon be forgotten?

Rabbi Simlai is apparently saying that every Jew comes into the world with a natural responsiveness to Torah teaching. Every Jew begins with a share in Torah that was vested in him before his birth, and though he is made to forget it, it is preserved in the deep recesses of his soul, waiting to be awakened by study and a favorable environment.... When a Jew studies Torah, he finds it native to his spiritual personality and he responds to it readily. It is an act of recollecting, recapturing, bringing

Rabbi Joseph B. Soloveitchik (1903–1993). Soloveitchik spent his formative years studying Torah in Lithuania and Belorussia. In 1926, he commenced his studies at the University of Berlin and wrote his dissertation on the epistemology and metaphysics of Hermann Cohen. In 1937, he founded the first Jewish day school in the New England area. In 1941, he became professor of Talmud at RIETS—Yeshiva University. In this capacity, he ordained more rabbis than anyone else in Jewish history. A remarkable orator, his annual Torah discourse, delivered on his father's *yahrtzeit*, attracted thousands of listeners. Among his published works are *Halakhic Man and Lonely Man of Faith*.

to the surface what was once learned and forgotten. The Torah did not impose upon the Jews some extraneous matter, foreign to their natures. Rather, Torah study and practice awaken the Jewish memory and we recall that which is inherent in the Jewish soul.

Rabbi Joseph B. Soloveitchik, *Reflections of the Rav* [Hoboken, N.J.: Ktav Pub. House, 1989], 1:60–61

Text 4a

רבי יהושע בן חנניה—אשרי יולדתו.

משנה, אבות ב,ט

Mishnah. The first authoritative work of Jewish law—with the exception of the biblical books—that was codified in writing. Due to the ongoing persecution of the Jewish people, it became increasingly difficult to guarantee that the oral traditions that were passed down from teacher to student would not be forgotten. Therefore, Rabbi Yehudah Hanasi, at the end of the 2nd century CE, redacted the Mishnah. The Mishnah supplements, complements, clarifies, and systematizes the commandments of the Torah. It is the central literary document that serves as the foundation for both the Jerusalem and Babylonian Talmud.

Praised be the woman who gave birth to Rabbi Yehoshua ben Chananyah!

Mishnah, Avot 2:9

Text **4b** 📜

ראה את רבי יהושע, וקרא עליו ״. . . זכור אני שהיתה אמו מולכת עריסתו לבית
הכנסת בשביל שיתדבקו אזניו בדברי תורה.״

תלמוד ירושלמי, יבמות א,ו

Rabbi Dosa ben Horkinas noticed Rabbi Yehoshua and said of him, ". . . I recall how his mother would bring his cradle to the study hall so that his ears would absorb the words of Torah."

Jerusalem Talmud, Yevamot 1:6

Jerusalem Talmud. Set up as a commentary to the Mishnah and compiled during the 4th and 5th centuries CE, the Jerusalem Talmud predates its Babylonian counterpart by 100 years and is written in both Hebrew and Aramaic. While the Babylonian Talmud remains the authoritative source for Jewish law, the Jerusalem Talmud remains an invaluable source for the spiritual, intellectual, ethical, historical, and legal traditions of Judaism.

Text **4c** 📜

כאשר תרגיל את הקטנים בתוך בתי מדרשות ירגילו עצמם לתורה. כמו שכתוב על
רבי יהושע, ״אשרי יולדתו״, כי תיכף כשנתעברה אמו לא זזה מבית המדרש, כדי
שישמע תמיד תורה, אף בעוד שהיה בבטן אמו.

פירוש הגר״א, שיר השירים א,ח

When children are accustomed to visiting the study halls, they will become more acclimated to the study of Torah. As it states regarding Rabbi Yehoshua, "Praised be the woman who gave birth to him"—because from the time she conceived, she did not budge from the study hall, so that her child would constantly hear words of Torah, even while in utero.

Rabbi Eliyahu of Vilna, Song of Songs 1:8

Rabbi Eliyahu of Vilna (1720–1797). Known as the Gra or the Vilna Ga'on; one of the greatest scholars of his day. In addition to Talmud, he excelled in all aspects of Torah study, including Kabbalah, and was proficient in secular subjects as well. He left a tremendous legacy, both from his writings on the Bible, Talmud, and Shulchan Aruch, and from the many students that he inspired to Torah and scholarship.

III. What's in a Name?
(Optional Section)

Text 5

הנה הנשמה עצמה קודם בואה בגוף אינה נקראת בשם כלל . . . נמצא השם אינו
לבחינת הנשמה עצמה, והרי גם לגוף עצמו אין השם מועיל. אך השם מקשר הנשמה
בגוף, והחיות הנמשך מהנשמה ומחיה הגוף הוא נשרש בהשם.

לקוטי תורה, בהר מא,ג

Rabbi Shne'ur Zalman of Liadi (Alter Rebbe/the Rav 1745–1812). Chasidic rebbe, halachist, and founder of the Chabad movement. According to family tradition, the Alter Rebbe was born in Liozna, Belorussia. He was among the principal students of the Magid of Mezeritch. His numerous works include the *Tanya*, an early classic containing the fundamentals of Chasidism; *Torah Or; Likutei Torah;* and *Shulchan Aruch HaRav*, an expanded code of Jewish law. He was succeeded by his son, Rabbi Dovber of Lubavitch.

Before a soul enters the body, it has no name. . . . The soul itself has no need for a name, nor does a [lifeless] body have any use for a name. Rather, the function of the name is to join the soul with the body; the vitalizing energy that emanates from the soul to give life to the body is rooted in the name.

Rabbi Shne'ur Zalman of Liadi, *Likutei Torah*, Behar 41c

Text 6

כאשר נולד האדם וקוראים לו אביו ואמו שם אחד העולה בדעתם, אינו באקראי
ובהזדמן, כי אם הקדוש ברוך הוא משים בפיו השם ההוא המוכרח אל הנשמה ההיא.

ספר הגלגולים, הקדמה כג

When a person is born and the father and mother decide to call this child by a name to which they both agree, it is not random or arbitrary. Rather, God places in their mouth the name that is needed for that soul.

Rabbi Chaim Vital, *Sefer Hagilgulim*, Introduction 23

Rabbi Chaim Vital (1542–1620). Lurianic Kabbalist and author. Rabbi Vital was born in Israel, lived in Safed, Jerusalem, and later Damascus. He was the principal disciple of Arizal, Rabbi Yitschak Luria, though he studied under him for less than two years. Before Arizal's passing, he authorized Vital to record his teachings. Acting on this mandate, Vital began arranging his master's teachings in written form, and his many works constitute the foundation of the Lurianic school of Jewish mysticism, which was later universally adopted as the Kabbalistic standard.

IV. Bar/Bat Mitzvah

Learning Interaction 1

If someone did not have a bar/bat mitzvah, what does he/she need to do?

a.   Arrange for a ceremony at the earliest possible opportunity

b.   Incorporate the ritual when he/she gets married

c.   Nothing

Text 7a

הקטן שהגיע לשלש עשרה שנה ויום אחד נעשה גדול, ומתחייב בכל המצוות
האמורות בתורה, ועד אותו זמן הוא קטן, שפטור מכל המצוות. וכן שנינו: בן שלש
עשרה למצות. שיעור זה של הזמן הוא הלכה למשה מסיני, כמו כל שיעורי תורה.
ויש שהסמיכוהו למקרא, שנאמר: ויקחו שני בני יעקב שמעון ולוי אחי דינה איש
חרבו, ולוי באותו פרק בן שלש עשרה שנה היה ונקרא איש.

אנציקלפדיה תלמודית, ערך בר מצוה

On his thirteenth birthday, a male is deemed mature and hence obliged to perform the *mitzvot* of the Torah. Until then, he is a minor and exempt from all *mitzvot*, as stated in the Mishnah: "Thirteen [is the age] for *mitzvot*." This age demarcation, like all measures, sizes, and quantities in Jewish law, was given to Moses at Sinai.

Some, however, have suggested scriptural support: The Torah says (Genesis 34:25), "Two of the sons of Jacob, Simeon and Levi, Dinah's brethren, took each man his sword." Levi at the time was thirteen years old and the Torah calls him "a man."

Talmudic Encyclopedia, entry "Bar Mitzvah"

Text **7b**

אימתי נעשית האשה גדולה . . . רבי סובר בת שתים עשרה שנה ויום אחד, אף על פי שלדעתו איש אינו נקרא גדול אלא בן שלש עשרה שנה ויום אחד. הלכה כרבי. וכשם ששיעור השנים של גדלות באיש כתבו ראשונים שהוא הלכה למשה מסיני, כך השעור י"ב שנה באשה הוא הלכה למשה מסיני.

אנציקלפדיה תלמודית, ערך גדולה

When does a female reach maturity? . . . Rabbi Yehudah says, on her twelfth birthday— though for a male it's on his thirteenth birthday. The Halachah is in accordance with Rabbi Yehudah.

Just as the age demarcation of thirteen for the male is a tradition from Sinai, the same is true for the age demarcation of twelve for the female.

Talmudic Encyclopedia, entry "Gedolah"

V. Marriage

A. Kidushin and Nisu'in

Learning Interaction 2

In your estimation, what are the three primary reasons that people seek marriage? Choose from the following list or add your own reason(s).

☐ Admiration

☐ Attachment

☐ Being part of a nuclear family

☐ Company

☐ Compatibility

☐ Emotional security

☐ Enjoyment

☐ Financial security

☐ Friendship

☐ Having children

☐ Love

☐ Meeting social expectations

☐ Passion

☐ Respect

☐ Satisfaction

☐ Serenity

☐ Sexual intimacy

☐ Shared purpose

☐ Tax benefits

☐ Trust

Text 8 📜

קודם מתן תורה היה אדם פוגע אשה בשוק, אם רצה הוא והיא לישא אותה,
מכניסה לביתו, ובועלה בינו לבין עצמו, ותהיה לו לאשה. כיון שנתנה תורה, נצטוו
ישראל שאם ירצה האיש לישא אשה יקנה אותה תחלה בפני עדים, ואחר כך תהיה
לו לאשה.

משנה תורה, הלכות אישות א,א

Before the Torah was given, when a man and woman would meet, and if both agreed to marry, he would bring her home, have marital relations in private, and thus she would be his wife.

When the Torah was given, God instructed the Jewish people that if a man wishes to marry a woman, he must first acquire her [hand in marriage] in the presence of witnesses, and afterwards she can become his wife.

Maimonides, *Mishneh Torah*, Laws of Marriage 1:1

Rabbi Moshe ben Maimon (Maimonides/Rambam, 1135–1204). Halachic authority, philosopher, author, and physician. Maimonides was born in Cordoba, Spain. After the conquest of Cordoba by the Almohads, he fled Spain and eventually settled in Cairo, Egypt. There, he became the leader of the Jewish community and served as court physician to the vizier of Egypt. He is most noted for authoring the *Mishneh Torah*, an encyclopedic arrangement of Jewish law, and for his philosophical work, *Guide for the Perplexed*. His rulings on Jewish law are considered integral to the formation of halachic consensus.

Text 9 📜

וכיון שנקנית האשה ונעשית מקודשת אף על פי שלא נבעלה ולא נכנסה לבית בעלה
הרי היא אשת איש . . . ואם רצה לגרש צריכה גט.

שם א,ג

Once the process of kidushin has been formalized, a woman is considered to be married even though the marriage has not been consummated and she has not entered her husband's home.... To dissolve this union, a *get*, a formal bill of divorce, is required.

Ibid., 1:3

Questions for Discussion

1. Why would the Torah mandate a period when the couple is married but may not enjoy a marital relationship?

2. What is marriage if not a relationship between a man and woman? In the absence of the relationship and what it has to offer, by what virtue is it marriage?

Text 10a

ברוך אתה ה׳ . . . אשר קדשנו במצותיו וצונו על העריות, ואסר לנו את הארוסות
והתיר לנו את הנשואות לנו על ידי חפה וקדושין.

ברכת אירוסין

Blessed are You, God . . . Who sanctified us with His commandments and instructed us [to refrain from engaging in] illicit relationships; He has forbidden unto us betrotheds and permitted unto us those whom we marry through chupah and [the preceding] kidushin.

Text of the Betrothal Blessing

היכן מצינו ברכה על השלילה, על מה שאסר לנו?

אבל באמת בשלילה זו יש החיוב הכי גדול. "ואסר לנו את הארוסות", שזאת אומרת כי היא ארוסה אף על פי שהיא אסורה, ועל כרחך שיש זיקה נפשית ורוחנית, זיקה אצילית ופנימית בין שני אנשים מבלי שום נגיעה ופניה חיצונית, שעל זה יש באמת לברך.

הגיונות אל עמי חלק ב', ע' מא

W here do we find the recitation of a blessing on a negative, on something that God forbade?

In truth, however, this "negative" isn't negative at all. The words, "He has forbidden unto us betrotheds" reveals a paradox: the woman is betrothed, yet she is forbidden to her husband. It must be then that the couple shares a profound soulful and spiritual bond that transcends any physical expression and is not contingent on external benefit. This, indeed, is reason to recite a blessing!

Rabbi Moshe Avigdor Amiel, *Hegyonot El Ami* 2:41

Rabbi Moshe Avigdor Amiel (1883–1946). Rabbi, religious thinker, author, and student of Rabbi Chaim Soloveitchik and Rabbi Chaim Ozer Grodzinski. A chief ideologue of religious Zionism, Amiel was elected chief rabbi of Tel Aviv in 1936. Amiel's first halachic publication was *Darchei Moshe,* followed by his three-volume *Hamidot Lecheker Hahalachah*. A renowned preacher, he published the homiletic works *Derashot El Ami* and *Hegyonot El Ami.*

Text 11

Rivkah Slonim. Scholar and lecturer, Slonim is the education director at the Chabad Center for Jewish Student Life at Binghamton University, one of the largest campus Chabad centers. Slonim co-authored the JLI course *Fascinating Facts* and is editor of *Total Immersion: A Mikvah Anthology* and *Bread and Fire: Jewish Women Find God in the Everyday*.

The mandatory monthly separation fosters feelings of longing and desire—at the very least, a sense of appreciation—which is followed by the excitement of reunion.

Over the course of a lifetime, open-ended sexual availability may well lead to a waning of excitement and even interest. The monthly hiatus teaches couples to treasure the time they have together and gives them something to look forward to when they are apart. Every month they are separated—not always when convenient or easy—but they wait for one another. They count the days until their togetherness, and each time there is a new quality to their reunion. In this regard the Talmud (Nidah 31b) states: "So that she will be as beloved as on the day of her marriage."

Rivkah Slonim, *Total Immersion: A Mikvah Anthology* [Northvale, N.J.: Jason Aronson, 1996], p. 32

B. Sinai Reenacted
(Optional Section)

Text 12 📜

"בְּיוֹם חֲתֻנָּתוֹ" (שיר השירים ג,יא), זו מתן תורה.

משנה, תענית ד,ח

"**O**n the day of His marriage" (Song of Songs 3:11): This refers to [the day of] the giving of the Torah.

Mishnah, Ta'anit 4:8

Text 13 📜

נקוט האי כללא בידך: כל המנהגים של חתן ושל כלה אנו למדין ממתן תורה, שה' היה מראה עצמו כחתן נגד כלה שהם ישראל.

תשב"ץ קטן תסה

The general rule is that all the customs regarding the bride and groom are learned from the giving of the Torah, when God appeared as a groom before His bride, Israel.

Rabbi Shimshon ben Tsadok, *Tashbets Katan 465*

Rabbi Shimshon ben Tsadok (13th–14th centuries). Author of *Tashbets Katan*, a halachic work. Most of the work is dedicated to documenting the rulings of his teacher, Maharam of Rothenburg. It is an important source for the halachic rulings of Ashkenazic Judaism. His work was cited extensively by later halachists and serves as the basis for many laws in the Shulchan Aruch.

Figure 4.2

Jewish Wedding Tradition	Parallel at Mount Sinai
Matches arranged by a shadchan	Moses was the middleman between God and Israel.
Wedding held in bride's hometown	Giving of the Torah here on earth, on "our" turf
Escorts of bride and groom hold candles.	Torches were seen at the giving of the Torah.
Groom breaks a glass beneath the wedding canopy.	Moses broke the tablets.
Entertaining the bride and groom with somersaults	That which was up came down; that which was down went up.
Marriage effected through a ring	God betrothed us with the Torah, which is akin to a ring.

VI. Death and Bereavement

A. Sacred Scroll

Text **14a**

העומד על המת בשעת יציאת נשמה חייב לקרוע. הא למה זה דומה לספר
תורה שנשרף.

תלמוד בבלי, מועד קטן כה,א

One who is present at the time of a person's passing is required to rend his clothing. This is because [a person's passing] is likened to the burning of a Torah scroll.

Talmud, Mo'ed Katan 25a

Questions for Discussion

Why is a person compared to a Torah scroll? What commonality do they share?

Text 14b 📖

Rabbi Yom Tov ben Avraham Asevilli (1250–1330). Spanish rabbi and author, known by the acronym Ritva; born in Seville; famous for his commentary on the Talmud. A student of the Rashba and Re'ah, he later assumed the rabbinate and became famous among Spanish Jewry. His commentary on the Talmud is known for its lucidity, and to this day is among the commentaries most frequently quoted and used.

והרמב״ן ז״ל פירש, שהנפש בגוף כאזכרות בגוילין.

ריטב״א, שם

Nachmanides, of blessed memory, explains that the soul in the body is like the inscription of God's names in the Torah scroll.

Rabbi Yom Tov ben Avraham Asevilli, ad loc.

Text 15 📖

כל מתעסק במת צריך לדעת שיש לו עסק עם דבר קדוש: גופו של אדם הוא לא רק נרתיק של קדושה ששמש לנשמה העילאית, אלא שהוא עצמו נתקדש גם בקדושה עצמית בדומה לספר תורה.

גשר החיים ה,א

Rabbi Yechiel Michel Tucazinsky (1874–1955). Born in Lithuania, his father died when he was still young. In 1882, his family settled in Israel and he studied in the Ets Chayim Yeshivah, where he eventually became the dean. Throughout the years, he published many books and articles on halachic issues, including *Hayomam Bekadur Ha'arets*, an effort to locate the halachic dateline. He was the first to publish an annual calendar that specified the laws and customs observed on each day.

All those who handle the dead must be aware that they are involved with a holy entity. The human body is not only the "container" that served the exalted soul, but has itself become sanctified with an independent holiness, similar to a Torah scroll.

Rabbi Yechiel Michel Tucazinsky, *Gesher Hachayim* 5:1

Text 16a

מת בעיר, כל בני העיר אסורין במלאכה.

שולחן ערוך, יורה דעה שמג,א

When a person dies, all the inhabitants of the city are forbidden to work.

Rabbi Yosef Caro, *Shulchan Aruch*, Yoreh De'ah 343:1

Rabbi Yosef Caro (Beit Yosef/Maran, 1488–1575). Scholar, author, and Sefardic halachic authority. Beit Yosef and his family fled Spain after the edict of expulsion of 1492 and eventually settled in Safed, Israel. He authored a commentary called *Beit Yosef* on the halachic work, the *Arba'ah Turim*. His magnum opus, the Shulchan Aruch (Code of Jewish Law), has been universally accepted as the basis for modern Jewish law.

Text 16b

ואם יש חבורות בעיר שכל אחת מתעסקת במתים ביומה, מותר ביום שאינה יומה.

שולחן ערוך, שם

If there are shifts in the city, with every shift tending to the dead on its designated day, then on their off-days, the members of the other shifts may work [even if there is a deceased person that needs to be cared for].

Rabbi Yosef Caro, ibid.

Text 17 📖

שמירת המת היא . . . משום כבודו. שאם יניחוהו לבדו, הרי זה כאלו עזבוהו ככלי אין
חפץ עוד בו.

גשר החיים ה,ד

We maintain a watch over the dead . . . out of respect. For if we were to leave the body alone, it would appear as if we abandoned it like a utensil that is no longer desired.

Rabbi Yechiel Michel Tucazinsky, *Gesher Hachayim* 5:4

Rabbi Moshe Sofer (1762–1839). Also known by the title of his main work, *Chatam Sofer*, a collection of responsa literature. One of the leading rabbinical authorities of the 19th century, his policies and decisions helped shape Austro-Hungarian Jewry. Born in Frankfurt am Main, Germany, he entered the yeshivah of Rabbi Natan Adler at the age of 9. After declining various offers for the rabbinate, he ultimately accepted a position in Pressburg (now Bratislava), Slovakia.

Text 18 📖

דכי בצלם אלהים עשה את האדם . . . אין חילוק בין ספר תורה שלם לאות אחת
ממנו, והוא הדין נמי עצם מעצמות הקדושים שנבראו בצלם אלהים אסור לנהוג בהם
מנהג בזיון.

שאלות ותשובות חתם סופר, יורה דעה שנג

Man was created in God's image. . . . Just as there is no difference between a complete Torah scroll and one letter from a Torah scroll [as both must be treated with utmost respect], it is forbidden to accord disrespect to even a single bone from sacred bodies that were created in God's image.

Rabbi Moshe Sofer, *Responsa Chatam Sofer*, Yoreh De'ah 353

B. Cremation

Text 19

כִּי הֹלֵךְ הָאָדָם אֶל בֵּית עוֹלָמוֹ, וְסָבְבוּ בַשׁוּק הַסֹּפְדִים . . .
וְיָשֹׁב הֶעָפָר עַל הָאָרֶץ כְּשֶׁהָיָה, וְהָרוּחַ תָּשׁוּב אֶל הָאֱלֹקִים אֲשֶׁר נְתָנָהּ.
קהלת יב,ה-ז

Man goes to his everlasting home, and the mourners go about in the street. . . . And the dust returns to the earth as it was, and the spirit returns to God Who gave it.

Ecclesiastes 12:5–7

Text 20

כִּי קָבוֹר תִּקְבְּרֶנּוּ בַּיּוֹם הַהוּא.
דברים כא,כג

You shall surely bury him on the same day.

Deuteronomy 21:23

Text 21 📜

מצוה לקיים דברי המת.

תלמוד בבלי, תענית כא,א

It is a mitzvah to uphold the wishes of the deceased.

Talmud, Ta'anit 21a

Text 22a 📜

אם צוה שלא יספדוהו אין סופדין אותו.

משנה תורה, הלכות אבל יב,א

If [the deceased] instructed that he should not be eulogized, then he is not to be eulogized.

Maimonides, *Mishneh Torah*, Laws of Mourning 12:1

Text 22b 📜

אבל אם צוה שלא יקבר אין שומעין לו.

משנה תורה, שם

If, however, he requested not to be buried, we disregard the request.

Maimonides, ibid.

C. Eternal Scroll

Text 23 📖

כתוב בעבודה זרה (דף יח) דשאלו תלמידים "מה אתה רואה?" ואמר להם, "גוילין נשרפים ואותיות פורחות באויר" . . . דהגויל הגשמי נשרף, והאותיות שהן רוחני פורחות למעלה . . .

והנה האדם מורכב מחומר וצורה, ובמות האדם לא מת רק חלק החומרי והגופני, והנשמה פורחת למעלה למקום אהלה שהיה שם בתחלה.

יד שאול, יורה דעה שמ,ה

It is related in the Talmud (Avodah Zarah 18a) that the students [of Rabbi Chananyah ben Teradyon] asked, "What do you see?" and he responded, "The parchment is burning and the letters are flying up in the air." . . . The physical parchment burned, and the letters, which are spiritual, flew up to heaven. . . .

A person, too, is comprised of matter and spirit. When a person dies, only the corporeal body dies, while the soul ascends to the place it originally inhabited.

Rabbi Yosef Shaul Natanson, *Yad Shaul*, *Yoreh De'ah* 340:5

Rabbi Yosef Shaul Natanson (1808–1875). Born in Berezhany, Poland; rabbi and authority on Jewish law. In 1857, he was elected rabbi of Lvov where he officiated for 18 years. His rulings, including his decision permitting machine-made matzah, are still widely cited. A wealthy man, Rabbi Natanson was also known for his activity as a philanthropist. He authored nine works on Jewish law and the Talmud, including *Me'irat Einayim* and *Sho'el Umeshiv*, a collection of his responsa. He is buried in Lvov.

Text 24 📖

צדיק אבד, לדורו אבד. משל לאדם שאבדה לו מרגלית, כל מקום שהיא מרגלית שמה. לא אבדה אלא לבעלה.

תלמוד בבלי, מגילה טו,א

When a righteous person is lost, he is lost to his generation. This can be compared to a person who lost a diamond. The diamond is lost to its owner; yet the diamond, wherever it may be, remains a diamond.

Talmud, Megilah 15a

Text 25 📖

המקום ינחם אתכם בתוך שאר אבלי ציון וירושלים.

נוסח ניחום אבלים

May God comfort you among the other mourners of Zion and Jerusalem.

Traditional text for comforting mourners

Text 26 🕮

נקודת נחמה אפילו באסון גדול כהאמור, ועוד יותר מנקודה,
מתבטאת בנוסח המסורתי והמקדש על ידי עשיריות דורות של תורה ומסורה של
עמנו—המקום ינחם אתכם בתוך שאר אבלי ציון וירושלים . . .
כמו שבנוגע לציון וירושלים שלטה יד הרומים, וקודם לכן יד הבבלים, רק בבית
המקדש הבנוי מעצים ואבנים כסף וזהב, אבל בית המקדש הפנימי שבלב כל אחד
ואחת של ישראל אין יד האומות יכולה לשלוט בו ונצחי הוא, כך הוא גם בנוגע לאבל
היחיד, אשר יד המות שולטת אך ורק בהגוף ועניניו, אבל הנשמה נצחית היא רק
שעלתה לעולם האמת.

אגרות קודש כ״ק אדמו״ר זי״ע כה, ע׳ ד-ה

Even in such a great tragedy, a modicum of solace—and even more than a modicum—is expressed in our traditional text of consolation to mourners, "May the Almighty comfort you among the other mourners of Zion and Jerusalem." . . .

The Romans—and the Babylonians before them—were able to destroy the Holy Temple of wood and stone, of gold and silver, but no nation can lay a hand on the inner "Holy Temple" in the heart of every Jew, for it is eternal.

The same applies to every personal loss. The hand of death can only touch the body and its concerns, but the soul is eternal; it has simply ascended to the World of Truth.

Rabbi Menachem Mendel Schneerson, *Igrot Kodesh* 25:4–5

Text 27 🕮

כמו שבודאי ובודאי יבנה השם חרבות ציון וירושלים ויקבץ נדחי ישראל מכל קצוי
תבל על ידי משיח צדקנו ויביאם ברנה לראות בשמחתה של ציון וירושלים, כך הוא
ללא ספק בנוגע לאבל היחיד, אשר יקיים ה׳ דברו "והקיצו ורננו שוכני עפר", ותגדל
השמחה, שמחה אמתית, בהפגשם כולם יחד בעת תחית המתים.

אגרות קודש, שם

We have perfect confidence that God will rebuild the ruins of Zion and Jerusalem; He will gather the dispersed remnants of Israel from the ends of the earth through our righteous Mashiach, and He will bring them in gladness to witness the joy of Zion and Jerusalem. We are equally confident that God will fulfill His promise that "those that dwell in the dust shall awake and rejoice" (Isaiah 26:19). Great indeed will be the happiness and rejoicing then, when all will meet together after the Revival of the Dead.

Rabbi Menachem Mendel Schneerson, ibid.

Lesson Summary

1. A birthday is a happy occasion from a Jewish-religious viewpoint, not only because it celebrates life but also because it celebrates a successful life. The soul yearns to fulfill its life mission, and there is no reason to presume that it will not be able to do so.

2. It is important for a birthday celebration to be associated with an increase in Torah and *mitzvot*. One thereby expresses how the purpose of his or her birth is already being actualized.

3. The fetus is taught Torah in utero so that the Torah will naturally resonate with the soul throughout life. Both God and the parents provide the fetus with the essential tools that will enable him or her to live a productive Jewish life.

4. Jewish mysticism teaches that the letters of the alphabet can be a conduit for spiritual energy. The energy that flows from the soul to the body is channeled through the letters of a person's name.

5. Because a name reflects a deep reality within a person, unless there is an important need, changing a name should be avoided.

6. Jewish mysticism teaches that the parents' naming of their child isn't arbitrary; God places the appropriate name for each soul into the parents' hearts.

7. At the age of bar/bat mitzvah, a child has the capacity and therefore the obligation to tell right from wrong and to act on this knowledge, though maturity of judgment will continue to develop for a long time to come. Even if these milestones slipped by without celebration, the change brought about by becoming bar/bat mitzvah has, in fact, occurred.

8. An underlying message in the Torah's story of the creation of Adam and Chavah is that when man and woman come together in marriage, irrespective of what initially attracted them to each other, their bond transcends benefits and favors; the two become one essential being.

9. Kidushin symbolizes the essential unity of the couple, because during the kidushin period, the marital relationship is not contingent upon any benefits. This period is not a void or absence; it is what allows the depth and beauty of marriage to be noticed.

10. The laws of family purity allow a couple to renew the excitement of marriage and experience the kidushin-nisu'in dynamic on a monthly basis. Furthermore, frequent "kidushin moments" enable us to properly cope with marital challenges.

11. Many Jewish wedding customs are derived from what occurred during the giving of the Torah, which was the wedding between God and the Jewish people.

12. The human body starts out as flesh and bones, but then the soul—the spark of God—is infused within the body, rendering the body itself a sacred entity. The body that housed the soul in life must continue to be treated with respect even after the soul has departed.

13. Jewish law dictates that the deceased be buried. Cremation is forbidden and is tantamount to a rejection of one of the fundamentals of Jewish faith, namely the resurrection of the dead that will take place in the time of the redemption.

14. Just as the inner Jerusalem in the heart of every Jew is impervious to destruction, the soul is eternal and continues to exist even after life has ended.

Additional Readings

Fetal Psychology

by Janet L. Hopson

Behaviorally speaking, there's little difference between a newborn baby and a 32-week-old fetus. A new wave of research suggests that the fetus can feel, dream, even enjoy *The Cat in the Hat*. The abortion debate may never be the same.

The scene never fails to give goose bumps: the baby, just seconds old and still dewy from the womb, is lifted into the arms of its exhausted but blissful parents. They gaze adoringly as their new child stretches and squirms, scrunches its mouth and opens its eyes. To anyone watching this tender vignette, the message is unmistakable. Birth is the beginning of it all, ground zero, the moment from which the clock starts ticking.

Not so, declares Janet DiPietro. Birth may be a grand occasion, says the Johns Hopkins University psychologist, but "it is a trivial event in development. Nothing neurologically interesting happens."

Armed with highly sensitive and sophisticated monitoring gear, DiPietro and other researchers today are discovering that the real action starts weeks earlier. At 32 weeks of gestation—two months before a baby is considered fully prepared for the world, or "at term"— a fetus is behaving almost exactly as a newborn. And it continues to do so for the next 12 weeks.

As if overturning the common conception of infancy weren't enough, scientists are creating a startling new picture of intelligent life in the womb. Among the revelations:

By nine weeks, a developing fetus can hiccup and react to loud noises. By the end of the second trimester it can hear.

Just as adults do, the fetus experiences the rapid eye movement (REM) sleep of dreams.

The fetus savors its mother's meals, first picking up the food tastes of a culture in the womb.

Among other mental feats, the fetus can distinguish between the voice of Mom and that of a stranger, and respond to a familiar story read to it.

Even a premature baby is aware, feels, responds, and adapts to its environment.

Just because the fetus is responsive to certain stimuli doesn't mean that it should be the target of efforts to enhance development. Sensory stimulation of the fetus can in fact lead to bizarre patterns of adaptation later on.

The roots of human behavior, researchers now know, begin to develop early—just weeks after conception, in fact. Well before a woman typically knows she is pregnant, her embryo's brain has already begun to bulge. By five weeks, the organ that looks like a lumpy inchworm has already embarked on the most spectacular feat of human development: the creation of the deeply creased and convoluted cerebral cortex, the part of the brain that will eventually allow the growing person to move, think, speak, plan, and create in a human way.

At nine weeks, the embryo's ballooning brain allows it to bend its body, hiccup, and react to loud sounds. At week ten, it moves its arms, "breathes" amniotic fluid in and out, opens its jaw, and stretches. Before the first trimester is over, it yawns, sucks, and swallows, as well as feels and smells. By the end of the second trimester, it can hear; toward the end of pregnancy, it can see.

Fetal Alertness

Scientists who follow the fetus' daily life find that it spends most of its time not exercising these new abilities but sleeping. At 32 weeks, it drowses 90 to 95% of the day. Some of these hours are spent in deep sleep, some in REM sleep, and some in an indeterminate state, a product of the fetus' immature brain that is different from sleep in a baby, child, or adult. During REM sleep, the fetus' eyes move back and forth just as an adult's eyes do, and many researchers believe that it is dreaming. DiPietro speculates that fetuses dream about what they know—the sensations they feel in the womb.

Closer to birth, the fetus sleeps 85 or 90% of the time: the same as a newborn. Between its frequent naps, the fetus seems to have "something like an awake alert period," according to developmental psychologist William Filer, Ph.D., who with his Columbia University colleagues is monitoring these sleep and wakefulness cycles in order to identify patterns of normal and abnormal brain development, including potential predictors of sudden infant death syndrome. Says Filer, "We are, in effect, asking the fetus: 'Are you paying attention? Is your nervous system behaving in the appropriate way?'"

Fetal Movement

Awake or asleep, the human fetus moves 50 times or more each hour, flexing and extending its body, moving its head, face, and limbs and exploring its warm, wet compartment by touch. Heidelise Als, Ph.D., a developmental psychologist at Harvard Medical School, is fascinated by the amount of tactile stimulation a fetus gives itself. "It touches a hand to the face, one hand to the other hand, clasps its feet, touches its foot to its leg, its hand to its umbilical cord," she reports.

Als believes there is a mismatch between the environment given to preemies in hospitals and the environment they would have had in the womb. She has been working for years to change the care given to preemies so that they can curl up, bring their knees together, and touch things with their hands as they would have for weeks in the womb.

Along with such common movements, DiPietro has also noted some odder fetal activities, including "licking the uterine wall and literally walking around the womb by pushing off with its feet." Laterborns may have more room in the womb for such maneuvers than first babies. After the initial pregnancy, a woman's uterus is bigger and the umbilical cord longer, allowing more freedom of movement. "Second and subsequent children may develop more motor experience in utero and so may become more active infants," DiPietro speculates.

Fetuses react sharply to their mother's actions. "When we're watching the fetus on ultrasound and the mother starts to laugh, we can see the fetus, floating upside down in the womb, bounce up and down on its head, bum-bum-bum, like it's bouncing on a trampoline," says DiPietro. "When mothers watch this on the screen, they laugh harder, and the fetus goes up and down even faster. We've wondered whether this is why people grow up liking roller coasters."

Fetal Taste

Why people grow up liking hot chilies or spicy curries may also have something to do with the fetal environment. By 13 to 15 weeks a fetus' taste buds already look like a mature adult's, and doctors know that the amniotic fluid that surrounds it can smell strongly of curry, cumin, garlic, onion and other essences from a mother's diet. Whether fetuses can taste these flavors isn't yet known, but scientists have found that a 33-week-old preemie will suck harder on a sweetened nipple than on a plain rubber one.

"During the last trimester, the fetus is swallowing up to a liter a day" of amniotic fluid, notes Julie Mennella, Ph.D., a biopsychologist at the Monell Chemical Senses Center in Philadelphia. She thinks the fluid may act as a "flavor bridge" to breast milk, which also carries food flavors from the mother's diet.

Fetal Hearing

Whether or not a fetus can taste, there's little question that it can hear. A very premature baby entering the world at 24 or 25 weeks responds to the sounds around it, observes Als, so its auditory apparatus must already have been functioning in the womb. Many pregnant women report a fetal jerk or sudden kick just after a door slams or a car backfires.

Even without such intrusions, the womb is not a silent place. Researchers who have inserted a hydrophone into the uterus of a pregnant woman have picked up a noise level "akin to the background noise in an apartment," according to DiPietro. Sounds include the whooshing of blood in the mother's vessels, the gurgling and rumbling of her stomach and intestines, as well as the tones of her voice filtered through tissues, bones, and fluid, and the voices of other people coming through the amniotic wall. Fifer has found that fetal heart rate slows when the mother is speaking, suggesting that the fetus not only hears and recognizes the sound, but is calmed by it.

Fetal Vision

Vision is the last sense to develop. A very premature infant can see light and shape; researchers presume that a fetus has the same ability. Just as the womb isn't completely quiet, it isn't utterly dark, either. Says Filer: "There may be just enough visual stimulation filtered through the mother's tissues that a fetus can respond when the mother is in bright light," such as when she is sunbathing.

Japanese scientists have even reported a distinct fetal reaction to flashes of light shined on the mother's belly. However, other researchers warn that exposing fetuses (or premature infants) to bright light before they are ready can be dangerous. In fact, Harvard's Als believes that retinal damage in premature infants, which has long been ascribed to high concentrations of oxygen, may actually be due to overexposure to light at the wrong time in development.

A six-month fetus, born about 14 weeks too early, has a brain that is neither prepared for nor expecting signals from the eyes to be transmitted into the brain's visual cortex, and from there into the executive-branch frontal lobes, where information is integrated. When the fetus is forced to see too much too soon, says Als, the accelerated stimulation may lead to aberrations of brain development.

Fetal Learning

Along with the ability to feel, see, and hear comes the capacity to learn and remember. These activities can be rudimentary, automatic, even biochemical. For example, a fetus, after an initial reaction of alarm, eventually stops responding to a repeated loud noise. The fetus displays the same kind of primitive learning, known as habituation, in response to its mother's voice, Fifer has found.

But the fetus has shown itself capable of far more. In the 1980s, psychology professor Anthony James DeCasper, Ph.D., and colleagues at the University of North Carolina at Greensboro, devised a feeding contraption that allows a baby to suck faster to hear one set of sounds through headphones and to suck slower to hear a different set. With this technique, DeCasper discovered that within hours of birth, a baby already prefers its mother's voice to a stranger's, suggesting it must have learned and remembered the voice, albeit not necessarily consciously, from its last months in the womb. More recently, he's found that a newborn prefers a story read to it repeatedly in the womb—in this case, *The Cat in the Hat*—over a new story introduced soon after birth.

DeCasper and others have uncovered more mental feats. Newborns can not only distinguish their mother from a stranger speaking, but would rather hear Mom's voice, especially the way it sounds filtered through amniotic fluid rather than through air. They're xenophobes, too: they prefer to hear Mom speaking in her native language than to hear her or someone else speaking in a foreign tongue.

By monitoring changes in fetal heart rate, psychologist JeanPierre Lecanuet, Ph.D., and his colleagues in Paris have found that fetuses can even tell strangers' voices apart. They also seem to like certain stories more than others. The fetal heartbeat will slow down when a familiar French fairy tale such as "La Poulette" ("The Chick") or "Le Petit Crapaud" ("The Little Toad"), is read near the mother's belly. When the same reader delivers another unfamiliar story, the fetal heartbeat stays steady.

The fetus is likely responding to the cadence of voices and stories, not their actual words, observes Fifer, but the conclusion is the same: the fetus can listen, learn, and remember at some level, and, as with most babies and children, it likes the comfort and reassurance of the familiar.

Fetal Personality

It's no secret that babies are born with distinct differences and patterns of activity that suggest individual temperament. Just when and how the behavioral traits originate in the womb is now the subject of intense scrutiny.

In the first formal study of fetal temperament in 1996, DiPietro and her colleagues recorded the heart rate and movements of 31 fetuses six times before birth and compared them to readings taken twice after birth. (They've since extended their study to include 100 more fetuses.) Their findings: fetuses that are very active in the womb tend to be more irritable infants. Those with irregular sleep/wake patterns in the womb sleep more poorly as young infants. And fetuses with high heart rates become unpredictable, inactive babies.

"Behavior doesn't begin at birth," declares DiPietro. "It begins before and develops in predictable ways." One of the most important influences on development is the fetal environment. As Harvard's Als observes, "The fetus gets an enormous amount of 'hormonal bathing' through the mother, so its chronobiological rhythms are influenced by the mother's sleep/wake cycles, her eating patterns, her movements."

The hormones a mother puts out in response to stress also appear critical. DiPietro finds that highly pressured mothers-to-be tend to have more active fetuses—-and more irritable infants. "The most stressed are working pregnant women," says DiPietro. "These days, women tend to work up to the day they deliver, even though the implications for pregnancy aren't entirely clear yet. That's our cultural norm, but I think it's insane."

Als agrees that working can be an enormous stress, but emphasizes that pregnancy hormones help to buffer both mother and fetus. Individual reactions to stress also matter. "The pregnant woman who chooses to work is a different woman already from the one who chooses not to work," she explains.

She's also different from the woman who has no choice but to work. DiPietro's studies show that the fetuses of poor women are distinct neurobehaviorally—less active,

with a less variable heart rate—from the fetuses of middle-class women. Yet "poor women rate themselves as less stressed than do working middle-class women," she notes. DiPietro suspects that inadequate nutrition and exposure to pollutants may significantly affect the fetuses of poor women.

Stress, diet, and toxins may combine to have a harmful effect on intelligence. A recent study by biostatistician Bernie Devlin, Ph.D., of the University of Pittsburgh, suggests that genes may have less impact on IQ than previously thought and that the environment of the womb may account for much more. "Our old notion of nature influencing the fetus before birth and nurture after birth needs an update," DiPietro insists. "There is an antenatal environment, too, that is provided by the mother."

Parents-to-be who want to further their unborn child's mental development should start by assuring that the antenatal environment is well nourished, low-stress, drug-free. Various authors and "experts" also have suggested poking the fetus at regular intervals, speaking to it through a paper tube or "pregaphone," piping in classical music, even flashing lights at the mother's abdomen.

Does such stimulation work? More importantly: Is it safe? Some who use these methods swear their children are smarter, more verbally and musically inclined, more physically coordinated and socially adept than average. Scientists, however, are skeptical.

"There has been no defended research anywhere that shows any enduring effect from these stimulations," asserts Filer. "Since no one can even say for certain when a fetus is awake, poking them or sticking speakers on the mother's abdomen may be changing their natural sleep patterns. No one would consider poking or prodding a newborn baby in her bassinet or putting a speaker next to her ear, so why would you do such a thing with a fetus?"

Als is more emphatic. "My bet is that poking, shaking, or otherwise deliberately stimulating the fetus might alter its developmental sequence, and anything that affects the development of the brain comes at a cost."

Gently talking to the fetus, however, seems to pose little risk. Fifer suggests that this kind of activity may help parents as much as the fetus. "Thinking about your fetus, talking to it, having your spouse talk to it, will all help prepare you for this new creature that's going to jump into your life and turn it upside down," he says—once it finally makes its anti-climactic entrance.

Psychology Today 31, no. 5 (1998):44
Reprinted with permission of the publisher

Get a Life!

by **Rabbi Yanki Tauber**

We Jews are a funny people. We celebrate the weirdest things. Everyone's heard of end-of-the-school-year parties, graduation parties, retirement parties. But who ever throws a get-to-work party?

Let me explain. Imagine that you have this dream job that's the envy of all your friends. Then, one day you receive a summons to the boss's office. The conversation goes something like this:

Boss: "Have a seat."

You: "Thank you."

Boss: "You've been here—what is it, twelve years now?"

You: "Yeah, it's almost that already. You guys take such good care of me . . ."

Boss: "We pay you a comfortable living wage, plus full health benefits, free day care and spa privileges, 31 days annual paid vacation . . ."

You: "Yes. I'm truly thankful."

Boss: "And what are your duties and responsibilities?"

You: "Nothing. Nada. Zilch. I've no duties or responsibilities."

Boss: "You don't even have to come to work, if you don't want to."

You: "Oh, but I do. Lots of times. It's fun. I hang around the office, see how things are done. Sometimes they even let me help out. You'd be surprised at how much I've learned. And I participate in all the company banquets and outings. I wouldn't miss those for anything . . ."

Boss: "Well, young lady, the party's over."

You: "W-what do you mean?"

Boss: "The party's over. Here, take this manual. It spells out your obligations . . ."

You: "Uh, it's sorta big and heavy. There must be almost a thousand pages in this book . . ."

Boss: "Actually, what you're holding in your hand is a very basic summary. The rest is in the library downstairs . . ."

You: "Oh, I know the library. There are tens of thousands of volumes there . . ."

Boss: "Well, we're doing important work here. And, starting tonight at sundown, you're going to be expected to be doing your part. You'll begin by following instructions, but to do your job right, you'll also need to understand the whys and the hows behind those instructions . . . You've picked up quite a bit in your time here, but we have guys who've been here all their adult lives and are still learning. Anyway, congratulations and good luck. I'll be watching your progress over the next 108 years . . ."

You: " . . . a hundred and eight years?"

Boss: "At least. Hopefully longer. Oh, by the way, don't forget to pick up your new ID tag at the front office on your way out."

After a conversation like that, would you run home and throw a party to celebrate? My daughter did. This week, she celebrated her Bat Mitzvah, the day that she became twelve years old.

A Bat Mitzvah is not an oversized birthday party. Leah's had eleven of those already. This is very different. What she celebrated was the fact that on the eve of her twelfth birthday she became *bat mitzvah* —a person who under Torah law is commanded, obligated and responsible to fulfill the mitzvot of the Torah.

She celebrated the fact that the Boss had called her into the office and told her that the party was over. Until now, she'd received everything her heart desired from Above and was not required to give anything in return. She was in learning mode—hanging around the office, picking up knowledge, getting a feel for how things are done. Now, she's a full-fledged employee, with a long list of duties and responsibilities. More than that—she's been made a partner in the company, fully responsible to make the enterprise work.

She's delighted. She threw a sumptuous party for her friends and family. We feasted, sang and danced and celebrated the event as the happiest day of her life to date.

It may be that life as a free lunch has its attractions. Very quickly, though, it becomes tedious and meaningless, forcing the free luncher to work harder and harder at all the contrivances that pump artificial meaning into life. But the fun leaks out faster than the most vigorous pumper can pump, leaving one deflated and defeated.

That's why we Jews don't throw retirement parties. Instead, we celebrate the day that we're handed the big fat book filled with duties and obligations and the ID tag that reads "Fully Responsible Member." Because we know that there is nothing more gratifying than being given a life that is truly our own.

Reprinted with permission of The Judaism Website, Chabad.org

A Jewish Wedding in 1787

by **Dr. Yitzchok Levine**

Dr. Benjamin Rush (1745-1813), a physician and a signer of the Declaration of Independence, "was the most striking, the most impressive, and the most controversial figure in North American medicine of his day. Brilliant and well educated, he was a restless soul, impatient and impulsive, quick to make decisions and to defend them against all disagreement. Nor did he confine his attention, solely to medicine: he was interested in every phase of life about him; and he was an ardent proponent of inoculation, and later, of vaccination, against smallpox. His work on mental illnesses was the standard for a half century."[1]

Dr. Rush was a prolific letter writer[2], and his letters give us keen insight into life during colonial times and after the Revolutionary War.

In 1787 Dr. Rush, who lived in Philadelphia, treated the family of Rebecca (Machado) and Jonas Phillips. On the morning of Tuesday, June 27, 1787, Mr. and Mrs. Phillips invited Dr. Rush, who was not Jewish, to attend the wedding of their daughter, Rachel, to Michael Levy, who was from Virginia. After attending the wedding Dr. Rush wrote a letter[3] to his wife, Julia, describing the *chasuna*. The reader will no doubt find it interesting to contrast the *chasuna* Dr. Rush attended with the *chasunas* of today:

I accepted the invitation with great pleasure, for you know I love to be in the way of adding to my stock of ideas upon all subjects. At 1 o'clock the company, consisting of 30 or 40 men, assembled in Mr. Philips' common parlor, which was accommodated with benches for the purpose. The ceremony began with prayers in the Hebrew language, which were chanted by an old rabbi

---

[1] http://dodd.cmcvellore.ac.in/hom/21%20-%20Benjamin.html

[2] *Letters of Benjamin Rush,* volumes I and II, edited by L. H. Butterfield, Volume I, 1761-1792, (Princeton, NJ: American Philosophical Society of Princeton University Press, 1951).

[3] Ibid., pp, 429-432.

and in which he was followed by the whole company. As I did not understand a word except now and then an Amen or Hallelujah, my attention was directed to the haste with which they covered their heads with their hats as soon as the prayers began, and to the freedom with which some of them conversed with each other during the whole time of this part of their worship.

As soon as these prayers were ended, which took up about 20 minutes, a small piece of parchment was produced, written in Hebrew, which contained a deed of settlement to which the groom subscribed in the presence of four witnesses. In this deed he conveyed a part of his fortune to his bride, by which she was provided for after his death in case she survived him.

This ceremony was followed by the erection of a beautiful canopy composed of white and red silk in the middle of the floor. It was supported by four young men (by means of four poles), who put on white gloves for the purpose. As soon as this canopy was fixed, the bride, accompanied with her mother, sister, and a long train of female relations, came downstairs. Her face was covered with a veil which reached halfway down her body. She was handsome at all times, but the occasion and her dress rendered her in a peculiar manner a most lovely and affecting object. I gazed with delight upon her. Innocence, modesty, fear, respect, and devotion appeared all at once in her countenance.

She was led by her two bridesmaids under the canopy. Two young men led the bridegroom after her and placed him, not by her side, but directly opposite to her. The priest now began again to chaunt a Hebrew prayer, in which he was followed by part of the company. After this he gave to the groom and bride a glass full of wine, from which they each sipped about a teaspoonful. Another prayer followed this act, after which he took a ring and directed the groom to place it upon the finger of his bride in the same manner as is practised in the marriage service of the Church of England. This ceremony was followed by handing the wine to the father of the bride and then a second time to the bride and groom. The groom, after sipping the wine, took the glass in his hand and threw it upon a large pewter dish which was suddenly placed at his feet. Upon its breaking into a number of small pieces, there was a general shout of joy and a declaration that the ceremony was over. The groom now saluted his bride, and kisses and congratulations became general through the room.

I asked the meaning, after the ceremony was over, of the canopy and of the drinking of the wine and breaking of the glass. I was told by one of the company that in Europe they generally marry in the open air, and that the canopy was introduced to defend the bride and groom from the action of the sun and from rain. Their mutually partaking of the same glass of wine was intended to denote the mutuality of their goods, and the breaking of the glass at the conclusion of the business was designed to teach them the brittleness and uncertainty of human life and the certainty of death, and thereby to temper and moderate their present joys.

Mr. Phillips pressed me to stay and dine with the company, but business and Dr. Hall's departure, which was to take place in the afternoon, forbade it. I stayed, however, to eat some wedding cake and to drink a glass of wine with the guests. Upon going into one of the rooms upstairs to ask how Mrs. Philips did, who had fainted downstairs under the pressure of the heat (for she was weak from a previous indisposition), I discovered the bride and groom supping a bowl of broth together. Mrs. Phillips apologized for them by telling me they had eaten nothing (agreeably to the custom prescribed by their religion) since the night before.

Upon my taking leave of the company, Mrs. Phillips put a large piece of cake into my pocket for you, which she begged I would present to you with her best compliments. She says you are an old New York acquaintance of hers.

During the whole of this new and curious scene my mind was not idle. I was carried back to the ancient world and was led to contemplate the Passovers, the sacrifices, the jubilees, and other ceremonies of the Jewish Church. After this, I was led forward into futurity and anticipated the time foretold by the prophets when this once-beloved race of men shall again be restored to the divine favor.

The Jewish Press, August 2, 2006
Reprinted with permission of *The Jewish Press*

Handle with Care

by **Devorah Leah Mishulovin**

Today I helped prepare Phyllis to meet her Creator.

"It is better to know us and not need us,
Than to need us and not know us."

That is what the plaque on the funeral home office door read. I thought that to be extremely strange. I can see this kind of philosophy at, say, a hospital or doctor's office. But at a funeral home?! It is inevitable; everyone is going to need them . . .

Oh well. I had some time to spare, and would have inquired about it within the office, but it was closed.

I sat on a bench instead, soaking in the peacefulness while waiting for the other volunteers to arrive.

Preparation of the dead for burial is undertaken by a community organization called the *chevrah kadisha*, the "Sacred Society." The volunteers of the Sacred Society quietly and privately wash, purify and dress the deceased, while simultaneously reciting lyrical prayers and Psalms.

We were a group of five women, eager to fulfill this mitzvah. This was my first time and I was a tad anxious. But this was something I had *wanted* to volunteer for, so I came with a positive attitude.

We walked into the room where the deceased woman lay completely covered. Her name, Phyllis, was scribbled on the wall-board.

Her name and the fact that she was Jewish were the only things I knew about her. Nothing else mattered.

The little bit of nervousness that I had felt dissipated when Tova, the leader of our group, uncovered Phyllis' face and remarked, "Oh, wow, she was a beautiful woman."

The atmosphere in the room was serene. There was a calm, a composure, a holiness.

There was a task to be done and our concern was accomplishing it with utmost dignity and care for the deceased, and of course according to the letter of the law.

Since I was the most inexperienced of the group, I chose to be the one to recite the special prayers as needed. However, as Tova began to guide us through the procedures, I felt myself able and willing to help hands-on.

There are many details involved in preparing and purifying the body before its burial. Laws and customs with symbolism and meaning; so special, so sacred. There is a system and order for every stage of the process. From the washing through to the dressing, from the preparing of the casket to placing the body inside. It is truly amazing how many details and beautiful rituals are involved in preparing the body for its next phase. From the sprinkling of soil from the Land of Israel, to the tying of the ribbons in the shape of a *shin*, (signifying G-d's name)—it is all a holy experience.

Again and again we were reminded to handle the body with gentleness, care and utmost dignity. Every movement was infused with such reverence, gentleness, it was awe-inspiring. I felt comforted knowing that I too, some day, will be treated with such respect.

This concept is what touched me so—the absolute honor given to the deceased. Keeping the body covered whenever possible. Moving the body gently and as little as possible. For example, when dressing the body in *tachrichim* (shrouds) we encountered some difficulty pulling down the shirt in the back. We wanted to lift the body, but Tova pointed out that we will be able to smooth everything out when we put the top shirt (*kittel*) on, and that way she will only be moved once.

It was a challenging task, after Phyllis was all dressed, to lift her off the table and to carefully place her into the *aron* (casket). Thank G-d through the team effort we managed without incident.

Lying peacefully in the *aron*, dressed in white, face covered, she was an awesome sight to behold, so pure, so holy, so ready to greet her Maker.

I felt comforted knowing that I too, some day, will be treated with such respect. After the *aron* was closed, we each apologized to Phyllis, in case we had moved her too quickly, a tad too roughly, or if by chance we mishandled or offended her in any way. I later learned that an annual fast day was established for the volunteers of this Sacred Society, as a form of repenting, if, G-d forbid, we had failed to handle with appropriate care.

So much care and attention to avoid hurting a *body*. The emphasis and caution to guard against offending someone who can no longer feel really altered my perceptions.

Made me think . . . more aware.

How we need to be ever so careful in treating our friends, neighbors and even total strangers who are alive. People with feelings, with sensitivities, troubles. Not because they can hurt you back, but because they are part of G-d.

If the Torah teaches us, with lots of intricate details, how to treat a body without a soul—without G-d's holy spark that gives it life, shouldn't we be so much more cautious and careful when relating to a human being *with* a soul?

"Phyllis the daughter of . . . . We ask forgiveness of you if we did not treat you respectfully.

May you be an advocate for all of Israel.

Go in peace, rest in peace, and arise in your turn at the end of days."

Reprinted with permission of The Judaism Website, Chabad.org

Adam and Eve

by **Rabbi Joseph B. Soloveitchik**

Aloneness and Loneliness

With his emergence, man-*persona* encounters another problem of the human situation. Now, after man has been burdened with the ethical, halakhic norm and has become a metaphysical being – only now *Hashem Elokim* decides to create Eve, the woman. Prior to being commanded, man-*natura* led a non-reflective, outer-directed, instinctive existence in union with his nature.

Hence, he did not face the specific human problem by which *homo-persona* is troubled. Of course, we all know what the problem is; the Torah has revealed it. "It is not good that the man be *levaddo*" (Gen. 2:18). *Levaddo* has a twofold meaning: aloneness and loneliness. Man as a rule dislikes both; does not want to be alone; he hates to be lonely. We understand very well that to be alone and to be lonely are two different problems. One may stand at Times Square where hundreds of people pass by every minute and yet feel very lonely. Vice-versa, one may find oneself, in terms of distance, in seclusion, very remote from people, without feeling lonely.

To be alone is, first, a physical fact and, second, a psychological condition which is not at all universal. Some people are loners; they prefer to be with themselves without being intruded upon by others. Of course, at times this urge to be alone assumes abnormal proportions, as in the case of reclusion. However, to retreat from society and to spend time apart from people is a frequent and normal exercise. Many like being alone. Of course, usually man is (as Aristotle knew) a gregarious animal; the herd instinct is powerful. He does not like to shut off the World from his life and, if compelled to do so, he feels miserable. Man-*natura* as a rule hates aloneness.

However, loneliness is not a physical fact, nor is it a most painful psychological condition. It is far more than that. Loneliness is a spiritual human situation. If I may say, it is an existential awareness or a metaphysical state, not only of the mind but of the soul as well. Loneliness reflects both the greatness of man as a unique metaphysical being, as well as his ontological insecurity as an incomplete being who, like a trapped animal, searches for an exit from his labyrinthine existence. It is both an inspiring as well as destructive experience. Lonely man is both hero and coward, giant and dwarf. There is anxiety as well as joy in the loneliness situation. However, it is only man-*persona*—introspective, meditating, and experiencing estrangement from nature—who is lonely. Metaphysical man finds himself in the throes of loneliness. Man-*natura*, who leads a gregarious, complacent, ebullient non-metaphysical existence, is not acquainted with this situation.

Man-*natura* suffers from aloneness, never from loneliness. He is outer-oriented and success-minded, thinks scientifically, and is not conscious of another ontological order beside the natural one. In loneliness, humans long for bliss and beauty, for a higher and more meaningful order, purged of evil, redeemed from contradiction and absurdity.

Let us pick up the verse, "It is not good that the man be *levaddo*." We have asked, what did *Hashem Elokim* mean by this dictum, aloneness or loneliness, for *levaddo* lends itself to either interpretation. The answer to this question is, I believe, to be found in the laconic five-word original Hebrew sentence. The Torah could have said, "*lo tov la-adam lihyot levaddo.*" However, it preferred the arrangement, "*lo tov heyot ha-adam levaddo.*" What is the difference between these two formulations? The first would read, if translated into the vernacular, "It is not good for the man to be *levaddo*"; the second, "It is not good that the man be *levaddo*." The first, had it been used by the Bible, would have expressed a utilitarian rule. A man alone cannot accomplish as much as two. He needs a helper from a utilitarian viewpoint. The second formulation, which the Scripture actually uses, has a different connotation: man's being *levaddo* is not good. This is an ontological postulate. A lonely human existence is not good; it lacks God's sanction and exposes an imperfect form of being. The helper whom God willed to make is indispensable not only for a pragmatic but for an ontological reason as well. Man needs help ontologically. Another homo-*persona* is necessary to complete man's existence, to endow it with existential meaning and directedness.

Marriage is not just a successful partnership, but an existential community. Adam and Eve met and a new metaphysical community, not just a successful partnership, was born. Had Adam needed a partner for practical reasons alone—to lighten his economic burden, to enable him to procreate, or to allow him a satisfactory sexual life—there would have been no necessity for the creation of Eve. We know from reading the first chapter that God created male and female. Both were endowed with great skill, talent, know-how and technical aptitude to control their environment. Male and female could have formed a dynamic, profitable partnership or company which would efficiently take care of all human needs, be they economic, physiological, or psychological. There was no need for natural man to meet Eve the woman, since he was already in company of the female who, for all practical purposes, would have made an excellent wife.

However, something had happened to man. The rendezvous with *Hashem* which resulted in man's encounter with the moral norm precipitated the birth of *homo-persona*, of a metaphysical man, of a singular spiritual personality. New man was burdened with a new awareness, one of inadequacy, illegitimacy and rootlessness; he was troubled by a great anxiety, by a sickness unto death—fright. In a word, he found himself lonely and forsaken. What he needed was not a practical partnership but an ontological community where his lonely existence could find completeness and legitimacy. The female of the first chapter did not qualify for that type of a community. A new woman had to be created, a woman who, like man, changed from a natural into metaphysical being, from female-*natura* into woman-*persona*, into a unique spiritual personality.

What is actually the difference between homo-*natura* and homo-*persona*? What is the main feature of the *persona* of metaphysical man? The Torah gives the answer in the story about naming the animals. The story appears to destroy completely the unity and continuity of the tale about the creation of Eve. However, the last sentence sheds light upon the link between this story and the emergence of Eve. "And the man gave names to all cattle and to the fowl of the air and to every beast of the field, but for Adam there was not found a helpmate for him" (Gen. 2:20). The story about Adam giving names to all cattle and fowl revealed to man the distinction between what he was prior to the command and what he became following it.

Man's Otherness from Nature

Adam named all the living creatures. What kind of a performance was it, and why did God encourage him to do this? It was a cognitive gesture. Sciences are divided into descriptive sciences (such as general botany, general zoology, geography and even astronomy) and explanatory sciences (such as physics). The job of the descriptive scientist is to introduce order into an allegedly chaotic world, to classify and generalize—their question is *what*. The explanatory scientists are concerned not with the *what* but with the *how*: Their question is, *how* do those objects function? Their prime instrument of cognition is the category of causality.

God wanted Adam to inquire into the what-ness of the world from a descriptive viewpoint. He encouraged Adam to classify and systematize a motley world which, at first glance, impresses us with its disorderliness and disarray. Primitive man saw no patterns in nature; he considered the latter replete with contradictions. Man started his progress by first introducing order into his environment, by classifying the fauna (and perhaps also the flora). This is the first scientific approach to nature: no magic, no spirit indwelling in every bush, no Golden Bough. Objective Adam approached his environment scientifically and tried to introduce orderliness.

At this point, there takes place man's breach with absolute, all-inclusive natural immediacy and his acquisition of a new capacity, that of turning around and facing the environment as something external and strange. Man, in order to become the ruler and developer of nature, must make an about face. Instead of marching naively with nature, he must suddenly stop moving along and encounter nature with the first question: what is it? When he begins to wonder what nature is and tries to understand it, he abandons the identity and unity of man and his environment and finds himself encountering it as a stranger and outsider.

At this point man discovers in himself an incommensurability with nature. He enters into a new phase in his emergence as a person: he views nature not from within but from without. While watching nature at a distance he gradually moves into a unique position of power and specific rights. The creative urge in man frees him from the state of all-out integration into one's environment.

Thus man experiences both oneness with and otherness from nature. He is an exponent of his kind, a representative of the group whose claim to existence is justified only at a generic level, and he is also an individual, a separate entity, who exists because he is himself, without being placed in a generic frame of reference. When man reaches the stage at which he is no longer a non-reflective being that forges ahead in unison with a mechanical-natural occurrence, but instead begins to single himself out in an act of confrontation with nature, he suddenly discovers in himself his own intelligence. He faces nature in a cognitive, critical, observant mood. The creative drive in him awakens in him curiosity and the desire for inquiry. The inquiry about the how, what and why, the quest for creativity comes to expression. Man begins to survey his environment and to uncover certain functional patterns of behavior.

When man breaks with immediacy and takes a look at nature from a distance, he encounters a reality which is not only outside of himself but also opposed to him. He is required to venture into an alien sphere. Aware of himself as an autonomous being capable of making decisions and charting a course of action, he also knows that the implementation of his decision depends upon something else, upon something outside of himself which can thwart the whole project he has conceived and organized. He must act, because God has implanted in him the urge to activate himself, and yet, at the same time, he cannot act, because he is removed from his exalted position as a subject and demoted to a mere object who bears consequences and is immobilized by the impact of events and things not of his making.

While Adam was busy describing, a great truth dawned on him. He realized that knowledge of the surrounding world by observation is gained by watching how the objects attracting our attention function. Objective observation is the source of knowledge of the world. However when it comes to man, observation alone will yield a very meager amount of knowledge. Man must confide in the person who is eager to understand him. Without confession there can hardly be an opportunity to learn why, who, and what a particular individual is. In order for man to be recognized, he must reveal himself; he must be interrogated and interviewed. The person whom I am eager to know must have confidence in the investigator, and be willing to state everything he knows about himself sincerely and truthfully. And even then the knowledge will not be complete, since many things are hidden from the eye of the person himself.

There is no depth to nature. Its existence is a flat two-dimensional one. The reality of nature exhausts itself in its functions. If you ask whether mute nature exists, I shall certainly answer "of course." However, if you continue to cross-examine me and ask me what I understand by existence, I will answer "activity." The existence of nature exhausts itself in its behavior, in its dynamics. There is nothing else to a mute existence. Hence, by watching the behavioral patterns, I gain an insight into the substance. Nature does not lie.

However man has an inner world; he exists inwardly as well as externally. Man's ontological essence, that is, the essence of his being, is not to be equated with his conduct or routine activities. There is a *homo absconditus*, a "hidden man" whom no one knows. He hardly knows himself. Hence in spite of watching man's activity we gain little knowledge. The latter is a mystery which no one can unravel. "All men are liars," says the Psalmist (Psalms 116:11). Not because they want to tell the untruth. They are simply unable to tell the truth. I see my neighbor every morning leave his house at 6:30; I know to where he drives off. I am also familiar with his occupation. I know what he will do when he will arrive at his place of business. I willy-nilly watched his conduct; I am acquainted with his habits and responses to certain challenges. I overhear his conversation with the members of his household, I know his concerns and interests. Do I know *him*? No, he is a mystery to me. The uniqueness of man-*persona* expresses itself in the *mysterium magnum* which no one except God can penetrate.

In order to escape loneliness, man-*absconditus* had to meet woman-mystery. They have a lot in common; otherwise Eve could not be a helper. However, they are also different; their existential experiences are incommensurate. The I-awareness in Adam is totally incomprehensible to Eve, and vice-versa. Each of them has a secret which neither will ever betray. Man-*persona* and woman-*persona* resemble each other and at the same time do not understand each other. She is *ezer kenegdo*, his helper and his opponent at the same time. For man and woman differ not only physiologically as male and female, of whom the first account of creation tells us, but also spiritually and personality-wise. This is the way in which the Creator has ordained human lonely destiny. Because the woman is not the shadow of man but an independent *persona*, because the woman projects a totally different existential image, her companionship helps man to liberate himself from his loneliness. In the interpersonalistic existential tension both man and woman find redemption.

Family Redeemed: Essays on Family Relationships
[Hoboken, NJ: Toras Horav Foundation, 2000], 15–22
Reprinted with permission of the publisher

Acknowledgments

We would like to thank all those whose dedicated efforts, individually and as a team, resulted in the present course, which has been presented by the Rohr Jewish Learning Institute (JLI) in over 350 cities worldwide.

We are especially grateful to **Mrs. Rivka Slonim** of **Chabad of Binghamton**, New York, and **Rabbi Avrohom Sternberg** of **Chabad of New London**, Connecticut, for developing the original course material and for their invaluable guidance based on their experience teaching this course on the ground.

Many thanks to **Rabbi Mordechai Dinerman**, the **lead editor** of the original course and the Sinai Scholars edition, for his constant attention to detail and his care and concern in ensuring the highest quality course material.

The many steps to publication have drawn upon the creative talents of many people. We are indebted to **Mrs. Chava Shapiro**, whose professional PowerPoint presentations added clarity and style to the course; to **Ms. Aviva Rozmaryn**, whose graphic design brought not only an artistic eye but also a scholarly one to the material; and to our copyeditor, **Mrs. Rachel Witty**, who meticulously prepared the manuscript for print. A special thank you to our Director of Marketing, **Rabbi Zalman Moshe Abraham**, for his eye-catching design of our book cover and marketing materials, and to **Ms. Rivka Dubov**, who creatively produced the promotional videos for the course.

A special thank you to the Sinai Scholars administrator, **Ms. Devorah Balarsky**, whose hardworking support and dedication to the Shluchim and all projects at Sinai Scholars Central is invaluable to our success and growth.

We are grateful for the expert guidance and experience offered by the Sinai Scholars curriculum committee: **Rabbi Shlomie Chein**, chairman; **Rabbi Mendel Matusof, Rabbi Mendy Zwiebel** and **Mrs. Bracha Leeds. Rabbi Eliezer Sneiderman** and **Rabbi Aaron Herman** gave us the benefit of their pedagogical training and input throughout production of the course.

Our editorial board provided their careful, professional review of the course material. Many thanks to **Rabbi Dovid Gurevich, Rabbi Eliezer Sneiderman** and **Rabbi Dov Wagner**.

The Sinai Scholars executive committee— **Rabbi Moshe C. Dubrowski, Rabbi Efraim Mintz, Rabbi Menachem Schmidt, Rabbi Nechemia Vogel, Mrs. Chana Silberstein, Rabbi Shlomie Chein, Rabbi Moshe L. Gray, Rabbi Dovid Gurevich, Rabbi Mendel Matusof, Rabbi Eitan Webb,** and **Rabbi Yisroel Wilhelm**—devote countless hours to the ongoing development of the Sinai Scholars Society. Their dedicated commitment and sage direction have helped Sinai Scholars continue to grow and flourish.

We especially offer gratitude to **Rabbi Efraim Mintz**, executive director of JLI, who is never content to rest on his laurels and who boldly encourages continued innovation and change.

Special mention is due to **Rabbi Levi Kaplan**, Director of Operations, and **Rabbi Dubi Rabinowitz**, Coordinator, for their ongoing efforts on behalf of Sinai Scholars and the JLI.

We are immensely grateful for the encouragement of our chairman, and vice-chairman of Merkos L'Inyonei Chinuch—Lubavitch World Headquarters, **Rabbi Moshe Kotlarsky**.

We are blessed to have the unwavering support of **Mr. George Rohr**, without whom Sinai Scholars itself would not be possible; since its inception, Sinai Scholars has been the recipient of Mr. Rohr's vision, care, concern, and support.

Finally, Sinai Scholars represents an incredible partnership of close to 70 campus shluchim who give of their time and talent with true self-sacrifice. They stand together on the front lines of the Rebbe's work, fighting Jewish indifference on college campuses across North America. We are truly privileged to partner in fulfilling our mandate of changing the face of the Jewish future.

Rabbi Shlomie Chein
UC S. Cruz, Chairman, Sinai Scholars Curriculum Committee

Rabbi Yitzchok Dubov
Director, Sinai Scholars Society

Sinai Scholars Society Chapters

AMHERST COLLEGE
Rabbi Shmuel Kravitsky

ARIZONA STATE UNIVERSITY
Rabbi Shmuel Tiechtel

BINGHAMTON UNIVERSITY
Rabbi Aaron Slonim

BIRMINGHAM CITY UNIVERSITY
UNIVERSITY OF BIRMINGHAM
Rabbi Yossi Cheruff

BOSTON UNIVERSITY
Rabbi Shmuel Posner

BRADLEY UNIVERSITY
Rabbi Eli Langsam

BROOKLYN COLLEGE
Rabbi Nachmon Wichnin

CALIFORNIA STATE UNIVERSITY, CHICO
Rabbi Mendy Zwiebel

CALIFORNIA STATE UNIVERSITY, NORTHRIDGE
Rabbi Chaim Shaul Brook

CARDOZO LAW SCHOOL
Rabbi Yechezkel Wolff

UNIVERSITY OF THE ARTS
Rabbi Daniel Grodnitzky

CLARK UNIVERSITY
Rabbi Mendel Fogelman

CONCORDIA UNIVERSITY
Rabbi Yisroel Bernath

CORNELL UNIVERSITY
Rabbi Eli Silberstein

DARTMOUTH COLLEGE
Rabbi Moshe Gray

DREXEL UNIVERSITY
Rabbi Chaim Goldstein

DUKE UNIVERSITY
Rabbi Zalman Bluming

EMORY UNIVERSITY
Rabbi Zalman Lipskier

FASHION INSTITUTE OF TECHNOLOGY
Rabbi Yaakov Werde

FLORIDA ATLANTIC UNIVERSITY
Rabbi Shmuel Liberow

FLORIDA INTERNATIONAL UNIVERSITY
Rabbi Levi Friedman

FRANKLIN AND MARSHALL COLLEGE
Rabbi Elazar Green

GEORGIA INSTITUTE OF TECHNOLOGY
GEORGIA STATE UNIVERSITY
Rabbi Shlomo Sharfstein

HARVARD UNIVERSITY
Rabbi Hirschy Zarchi

HOFSTRA UNIVERSITY
NASSAU COMMUNITY COLLEGE
Rabbi Shmuel Lieberman

INDIANA UNIVERSITY
Rabbi Yehoshua Chincholker

JOHNS HOPKINS UNIVERSITY
Rabbi Zev Gopin

LEHIGH UNIVERSITY
Rabbi Zalman Greenberg

McGILL UNIVERSITY
CONCORDIA UNIVERSITY
Rabbi Shmuel Weiss

NEW YORK UNIVERSITY
Rabbi Dov Yona Korn

NORTHERN ARIZONA UNIVERSITY
Rabbi Dovie Shapiro

NORTHWESTERN UNIVERSITY
Rabbi Dov Hillel Klein

OHIO STATE UNIVERSITY
Rabbi Zalman Deitsch

PENN STATE UNIVERSITY
Rabbi Nosson Meretsky

PRATT INSTITUTE
Rabbi Simcha Weinstein

PRINCETON UNIVERSITY
Rabbi Eitan Webb

QUEEN'S UNIVERSITY
Rabbi Yisroel Simon

QUEENS COLLEGE
Rabbi Shaul Wertheimer

REED COLLEGE
Rabbi Dov Bialo

S. DIEGO STATE UNIVERSITY
Rabbi Chalom Boudjnah

S. FRANCISCO STATE UNIVERSITY
Rabbi Yisroel Zaetz

S. MONICA COLLEGE
Rabbi Moshe Levitansky

STANFORD UNIVERSITY
Rabbi Dov Greenberg

SUNY BUFFALO
Rabbi Avrohom Gurary

SUNY NEW PALTZ
Rabbi Moshe Plotkin

SUNY ONEONTA
Rabbi Meir Simcha Rubashkin

SUNY Oswego
Rabbi Yossi Madvig

SUNY Stony Brook
Rabbi Adam Stein

Swarthmore College
Haverford College
Rabbi Eli Gurevitz

Temple University
Rabbi Baruch Shalom Kantor

Texas A&M
Rabbi Yossi Lazaroff

The College of New Jersey
Rabbi Kivi Greenbaum

Towson University
Goucher College
Rabbi Mendy Rivkin

Tufts University
Rabbi Tzvi Backman

Tulane University
Rabbi Yochanan Rivkin

UCLA
Rabbi Dovid Gurevich

Union College
Rabbi Shmully Rubin

Universities of Berlin
Rabbi Tzvi Greenberg

University of Arizona
Rabbi Yossi Winner

University of California, Berkeley
Rabbi Gil Leeds

University of California, Irvine
Rabbi Zevi Tenenbaum

University of California, S. Barbara
Rabbi Mendel Loschak

University of California, S. Cruz
Rabbi Shlomie Chein

University of California, S. Diego
Rabbi Yehuda Hadjadj

University of Central Florida
Rabbi Chaim Baruch Lipskier

University of Chicago
Rabbi Yossi Brackman

University of Colorado
Rabbi Yisroel Wilhelm

University of Connecticut
Rabbi Shlomo Hecht

University of Delaware
Rabbi Eliezer Sneiderman

University of Florida, Gainesville
Rabbi Berl Goldman

University of Georgia
Rabbi Michoel Refson

University of Hartford
Rabbi Yosef Kulek

University of Illinois at Chicago
Rabbi Benzion Shemtov

University of Illinois at Urbana Champaign
Rabbi Dovid Tiechtel

University of Kansas
Rabbi Zalman Tiechtel

University of Maryland
Rabbi Eli Backman

University of Massachusetts
Rabbi Chaim Adelman

Universities of Melbourne
Rabbi Moshe Weiss

University of Miami
Rabbi Mendy Fellig

University of Milwaukee
Rabbi Yechezkel Thaler

University of Minnesota
Rabbi Yitzi Steiner

University of Missouri
Rabbi Avraham Lapine

University of Nevada, Las Vegas
Rabbi Tzvi Bronchtain

University of Ottawa
Rabbi Chaim Boyarsky

University of Oxford
Rabbi Eli Brackman

University of Pennsylvania
Rabbi Levi Haskelevich

University of Pittsburgh
Rabbi Shmuel Weinstein

University of Rochester
Rabbi Asher Yaras

University of Southern California
Rabbi Dov Wagner

University of Texas at Austin
Rabbi Zev Johnson

University of Toronto
Rabbi Yeshaya Rose

University of Vermont
Rabbi Zalman Wilhelm

University of Virginia
Rabbi Shlomo Mayer

University of Washington
Rabbi Elie Estrin

University of Wisconsin
Rabbi Mendel Matusof

University of South Florida, Tampa
Rabbi Pinny Backman

Vanderbilt University
Rabbi Shlomo Rothstein

Virginia Tech
Rabbi Zvi Zwiebel

Washington University
Rabbi Hershey Novack

Waterloo University
Rabbi Moshe Goldman

Wesleyan University
Rabbi Levi Schectman

Western Washington University
Rabbi Avremi Yarmush

York University
Rabbi Vidal Bekerman

SINAI SCHOLARS SOCIETY

a joint project of
Chabad on Campus
and **The Rohr Jewish Learning Institute**

Chabad
on Campus

Chairman
Rabbi Moshe Kotlarsky
Lubavitch World Headquarters, New York

Sinai Scholars Society Executive Committee
Rabbi Menachem Schmidt
Chairman
Philadelphia , PA

Rabbi Nechemia Vogel
Rochester, NY

Rabbi Efraim Mintz
Brooklyn, NY

Rabbi Moshe Chaim Dubrowski
Chabad on Campus
International Foundation
Brooklyn, NY

Dr. Chana Silberstein
Ithaca, NY

Rabbi Shlomie Chein
University of California S. Cruz

Rabbi Moshe L. Gray
Dartmouth College

Rabbi Dovid Gurevich
UCLA

Rabbi Mendel Matusof
University of Wisconsin

Rabbi Eitan Webb
Princeton University

Rabbi Yisroel Wilhelm
University of Colorado

Director, Sinai Scholars Society
Rabbi Yitzchok Dubov
Brooklyn, NY

Administrator
Ms. Devorah Balarsky
Brooklyn, NY

JLI Director
Rabbi Efraim Mintz
Brooklyn, NY

Director of Operations
Rabbi Levi Kaplan

Special Projects Coordinator
Rabbi Dubi Rabinowitz

JLI Executive Committee
Rabbi Chaim Block
S. Antonio, TX

Rabbi Hesh Epstein
Columbia, SC

Rabbi Yosef Gansburg
Toronto, ON

Rabbi Shmuel Kaplan
Potomac, MD

Rabbi Yisrael Rice
S. Rafael, CA

Rabbi Avrohom Sternberg
New London, CT

Authors
Dr. Shmuel Klatzkin
Dayton, OH

Rabbi Moshe Miller
Chicago, IL

Rabbi Eli Silberstein
Ithaca, NY

Mrs. Shimonah Tzukernik
Brooklyn, NY

Editorial Board
Rabbi Benny Rapoport
Clarks Summit, PA

Rabbi Berel Bell
Montreal, QC

Rabbi Eli Silberstein
Ithaca, NY

Rabbi Shmuel Posner
Boston, Massachusetts

Rabbi Eliezer Sniederman
Newark, Delaware

Rabbi Dov Wagner
Los Angeles, CA

Rabbi Dovid Gurevich
UCLA

Developmental Editors
Rabbi Mordechai Dinerman
Brooklyn, NY

Rabbi Naftali Silberberg
Brooklyn, NY

Research Assistants
Rabbi Shaul Goldman
Brooklyn, NY

Rabbi Binyomin Walters
Brooklyn, NY

Curriculum Committee
Rabbi Shlomie Chein
University of California S. Cruz

Rabbi Mendel Matusof
University of Wisconsin

Rabbi Mendy Zweibel
University Of California, Chico

Mrs. Bracha Leeds - Consultant
University Of California, Berkeley

National Retreat Committee
Rabbi Dov Hillel Klein
Northwestern University

Rabbi Zalman Lipskier
Emory University

Rabbi Eliezer Sniederman
University of Delaware

Made in United States
North Haven, CT
02 May 2022